CHATTEL SLAVERY
AND WAGE SLAVERY

CHATTEL SLAVERY

AND

WAGE SLAVERY

The Anglo-American Context
1830–1860

MARCUS CUNLIFFE

MERCER UNIVERSITY
LAMAR MEMORIAL LECTURES
No. 22

THE UNIVERSITY OF GEORGIA PRESS

ATHENS

Set in 11 on 15 point Mergenthaler Baskerville type
Printed in the United States of America

Library of Congress Cataloging in Publication Data

Cunliffe, Marcus.
    Chattel slavery and wage slavery.
    (Mercer University Lamar memorial lectures; no.
22)
    Includes bibliographical references and index.
    1. Slave labor—Southern States—History.   2. La-
bor and laboring classes—United States—History.
3. Slavery in the United States—Economic aspects—
Southern States—History.   I. Title.   II. Title: Wage
slavery.   III. Series: Mercer University, Macon, Ga.
Lamar memorial lectures; v. 22.
HD4865.U6C86   331.1'17   78-27195
            ISBN 0-8203-0471-9

FOR KEITH AND SUSAN
AND THEIR
ANGLO-AMERICAN CONTEXT

Contents

Foreword

FOR MORE THAN TWO DECADES MERCER UNIVERSITY HAS been bringing renowned scholars to its campus to deliver the annual Lamar Memorial Lectures. Until now all have been American scholars. As required by the Lamar trust, they have explored the vast domain of southern history and culture with whatever advantages may have accrued to them as native Americans. Over the years these visitors have built an impressive body of literature addressed to the complexities of southern history and culture, or, as some would say, the southern mystique.

Several years ago the Lamar Memorial Lectures Committee, caught up in the spirit of the Bicentennial celebration, began to explore the possibilities of introducing a transatlantic point of view into the series. The prospect of an "outside" look into the South's past promised to be both interesting and instructive. The result of this decision was to extend a lecture invitation to the internationally recognized scholar Professor Marcus Cunliffe, of the University of Sussex, England. By happy coincidence Professor Cunliffe was to be in this country in 1977–78 as a fellow of the Woodrow Wilson Center in Washington, D.C. The invitation was accepted and these published lectures were delivered in an abbreviated form on the Mercer University campus, Macon, Georgia, in April 1978.

Somewhat surprisingly Professor Cunliffe chose to lecture on American slavery, specifically the debate over abolition. The announcement of his intent to survey this perennially fascinating topic by considering not only the North and the South but also Great Britain aroused considerable anticipation and we were not disappointed. Although his lectures are filled with a variety of insights into the abolitionist issue, the thrust of his argument is that any analysis of the abolitionist movement must incorporate the wage and class themes of the era, which were not properly considered by opponents of chattel slavery in either England or the United States. Moreover these matters cannot be disentangled from the Anglo-American tensions of the times, and the complex manner in which these tensions impinged on the abolitionist debate is explored in some depth by Professor Cunliffe in the life and career of Charles Edwards Lester. Modern scholars are thus left to ponder once again the exact nature and meaning of one of this country's most turbulent reform movements and the forces that swirled in and about the stormy confrontation.

In her will creating this lectureship Mrs. Eugenia Dorothy Blount Lamar sought to establish a lecture series of the highest quality which would explain and preserve southern life and culture. Professor Cunliffe has more than fulfilled these exacting requirements.

And there was a welcomed bonus: Professor Cunliffe's personal charm and warmth, his relaxed and uncomplicated friendliness, and his keen wit and erudition were a joy to all who came to know him and will long be remembered on the Mercer campus.

Henry Y. Warnock, Chairman
Lamar Memorial Lectures Committee

Mercer University
Macon, Georgia

Preface

I THINK I AM THE FIRST ENGLISHMAN, INDEED THE FIRST non-American, to have delivered the Lamar Memorial Lectures in Mercer University's well-established annual series. The honor, I felt, also conferred a certain burden of responsibility. It seemed right to choose a theme linking the history of my own country with that of the American South. But a number of difficulties lie in the way of such an endeavor. It is arguable that ancestry, social attitudes, and trade patterns combine to have made the historic South the most "British" region of the United States. Yet a recital of these ties, in a spirit of transatlantic bonhomie, would have been more suitable to a short after-dinner speech than to the scholarly demands of the Lamar Lectures. There would have been a risk of sentimental distortion. For, after all, my countrymen have tended to regard the United States as a single entity, not as a nation rigidly divided between North and South; they have often expressed severe disapproval of American doings, North and South; and Americans in return have often denounced British behavior. Cordiality has been accompanied by mutual recrimination. We hold "hands across the sea," yes, and at times with heartfelt amity; but at other times in the past the hands were, so to speak, encased in boxing gloves.

In the interests of genuine historical understanding, and in consultation with the Lectures Committee, I decided upon a comparative approach to the multiple concepts of "slavery" during the period from 1830 to 1860. This would not focus exclusively upon Anglo-Southern relations, and it would in part be a story of stereotypes and prejudices. The aim was to show how, why, and with what effect the chattel slavery of the antebellum era was viewed in relation to the "wage" or "white" slavery of workers elsewhere—in the Northern states, and especially in Great Britain or in territories under British control.

There is a vast literature dealing with chattel slavery as a labor system. There is also a vast literature, Marxist and otherwise, that reverses the terms and defines supposedly "free" systems of labor as in themselves a type of slavery, since these systems are perceived as coercive and exploitative. In between stretches an ambiguous terrain, a jumble of theories about poverty, work, economic necessity, and racial characteristics. One deeply held Anglo-American conviction, whose roots go back at least as far as Elizabethan England, is that some people are lazy and shiftless, and if left to their own devices would become rogues and beggars—a menace and an expense to the community. Satan, in the words of the old proverb, finds mischief for idle hands to do. Accordingly, it was believed that people must be obliged to work, for their own good and that of society. A corollary was that, if thrown out of work, the "deserving poor" would soon find fresh employment. In any case, neither they nor the "undeserving poor" ought to be given more than the barest minimum of unemployment relief. "Idle" and "unemployed" became closely synonymous.

These assumptions were held to apply to all laborers, irrespective of age, sex, or color. Resistance to slave emancipation in the era of the American Revolution was thus based upon a universal economic dogma, though no doubt reinforced by particular racial biases. Thomas Jefferson and his Virginia contemporary, St. George Tucker, feared that emancipated slaves might constitute an "idle, dissipated and finally a numerous banditti, instead of turning their attention to industry and labour." As Edmund S. Morgan reports in *The Challenge of the American Revolution*, Tucker wanted free blacks "*bound* to labour," if need be. Imperatives not much less stern were invoked for white artisans in nineteenth-century Britain and America. In fact, long hours of work, regularity of attendance, and the use of female and child labor acquired increasing sanction with the spread of large-scale, complex manufacturing. "Free" labor thus became more regimented, and in many industries less "manly." This process was more and more apparent, at least to the articulate poor and to radical theorists, by about 1830.

It was, however, paralleled, and implicitly negated (also from about 1830), by an optimistic rhetoric, a vision of release from drudgery via technology and of decent prosperity by means of hard work and self-help.

Essayists and sermonizers declared that the laborer was worthy of his hire and should take pride in his calling. They spoke of the dignity of labor. In the United States still more than in Britain, though, the moral was not altogether clear. Labor was praised as an ennobling task, a self-imposed discipline, irrespective of the discipline imposed by the factory hooter. On the other hand, the presumption was that the workingman would justify his activity by raising himself out of the ranks of the laboring class. He would prove his merit by emerging as an employer instead of an employee. If he remained a laborer, was he then a failure? If he himself was a failure, could his status properly be deemed dignified?

A third element, also conspicuous from about 1830 and consorting uneasily with the other two, was the fierce new Anglo-American abolitionist campaign for immediate emancipation. The "immediatists" insisted that chattel slavery was a brutal, immoral, and economically retrograde anomaly, utterly at odds with the democratic creed of individual liberty within a Christian polity. After 1830 the three doctrines began to impinge upon one another with mounting urgency and confusion.

Here then is an intricate subject, international in scope and involving Britain and the United States in a tangle of controversy. Within the compass of these lectures, I could of course not hope to be exhaustive. I have not sought to weigh the actual validity—economic, social, moral—of the comparison between chattel slavery and wage slavery. I have not, for example, considered whether antislavery propaganda exaggerated the miseries of plantation workers, or whether British (and Northern) artisans could in any precise sense be categorized as "slaves." The titles and commentary in the notes may help the reader to pursue such inquiries in the work of David B. Davis and numerous other erudite and imaginative historians.

The pages that follow are an expanded version of the lectures I was privileged to present at Mercer in April 1978. Of the trio, the opening lecture outlines the evolution of the notion of wage slavery in Europe and the United States, and suggests its importance as a factor affecting assessments—favorable, critical, or neutral—of chattel slavery. The next portion discusses the touchiness of Anglo-American relationships—the product of a common heritage, old antagonisms, stylized antitheses, and emulative rivalry. The thesis is that, in their resentment of "mother-country" rebukes, Americans were provoked into the retaliatory claim that British wage slavery was more deplorable than plantation slavery; and that using monarchical Britain as a supposed antithesis to republican America encouraged Americans, North and South, to evade uncomfortable domestic problems, concerning not only chattel slavery but the growth of a substantial, indigenous industrial work force. The divisive, obfuscating, yet in a way nonsectional aspects of the "black slavery"–"white slavery" quarrel are, finally, illustrated by charting the career of a now-obscure but perhaps significant Northerner, Charles Edwards Lester. Lester, initially an abolitionist, joined with other Americans in concluding that the real villains of the antebellum world were not the vigorous planters of the South but a scheming, anti-American coalition of British aristocrats and manufacturers, determined to destroy the Republic.

The material I offered at Mercer University was, as this summary may indicate, in its nature somewhat intractable, speculative and even perverse. My audience was nevertheless courteous and responsive, assisting me at several points to clarify issues and document them. Dr. Carlos Flick was particularly helpful. I much enjoyed my stay in Macon; Professor Henry Warnock and his colleagues demonstrated that, in whatever other respects the present-day South may be altering, the tradition of hospitality survives unimpaired.

In addition to those mentioned in the notes, I have profited from the research and advice of W. H. Chaloner, Howard Temperley, Jonathan Glickstein, Phyllis Palmer, and John F. C. Harrison. I have benefited from the opportunity to exchange ideas with Michael Kammen and his associates at Cornell University, and with other historians at Georgetown University and the Graduate School, City University of New York. I am obliged to the Library of Congress and the New-York Historical Society for permission to reproduce two cartoons which graphically depict my theme. And finally, I gained rich advantages—companionship, aid in research (from Wendell Franklin and Chauncey B. Jessop), the borrowing of books, the typing of the manuscript—from a 1977–78 fellowship at the Wood-row Wilson International Center for Scholars, housed in the old Smithsonian "Castle" in Washington, D.C.

Marcus Cunliffe

Washington, D.C.
June 1978

CHATTEL SLAVERY
AND WAGE SLAVERY

ONE

Slavery, "Black" and "White"

EVERYONE INTERESTED IN THE OLD SOUTH KNOWS THAT its "peculiar institution," chattel slavery, was justified in a number of different ways. Of these justifications, perhaps the trickiest to deal with rested upon how the term *slavery* should be interpreted. In brief, the Southern case was that slavery—properly defined—was not in fact "peculiar" to the South, but a fundamental feature of Great Britain and, to a growing extent, of the states north of Mason and Dixon's line.

Historians usually regard George Fitzhugh of Virginia as the most beguiling Southern polemicist to insist on a comparative approach. In the essays published as *Sociology for the South* (1854) and *Cannibals All!* (1857), Fitzhugh claimed that slavery was a universal tendency, and that plantation slavery was more humane than the industrial conscription of the supposedly "free" labor market. What he called "the White Slave Trade," by which he meant the whole apparatus of the economic order, was in Fitzhugh's opinion "far more cruel than the Black Slave Trade, because it exacts more of its slaves, and neither protects nor governs them." Modern industrial society, said Fitzhugh, boasted that the profits of free labor were greater than those from slave labor. This could only mean that the employer of free labor paid less, directly or indirectly, to his employees. The "freedom" of white workers was thus illusory. They were obliged to begin work as children; they were discarded when business was slack, or when sickness, disability, or old age overtook them.[1]

The same comparison, emphatically in favor of the South, was drawn in a long poem also familiar to students of the antebellum period: *The Hireling and the Slave* (1855), by William J. Grayson of Charleston, South Carolina. The South, in Grayson's idyllic picture, was a contented region. The plantation slave was fed, clothed, and housed from the cradle to the grave. The "hireling" of Grayson's title, on the other hand, though paid wages, was a slave in desperate straits. "Hirelingism" was a brutal system that forced men, women, and children into ill-paid, hopeless drudgery; and the vilest conditions were to be found in the mother country. Here is the English scene, sketched in the neat couplets of Grayson's poem:

> With no restraint but what the felon knows,
> With the sole joy that beer or gin bestows,
> To gross excess and brutalizing strife,
> The drunken hireling dedicates his life:
> Starved else, by infamy's sad wages fed,
> There women prostitute themselves for bread,
> And mothers, rioting with savage glee,
> For murder'd infants spend the funeral fee;

Childhood bestows no childish sports or toys,
Age neither reverence nor repose enjoys,
And want and suffering only end with life;
In crowded huts contagious ills prevail,
Dull typhus lurks, and deadlier plagues assail,
Gaunt Famine prowls around his pauper prey,
And daily sweeps his ghastly hosts away;
Unburied corses taint the summer air,
And crime and outrage revel with despair.

On Southern plantations, however, in Grayson's version, "The slave escapes the perils of the poor."[2]

This apparent paradox, of carefree slavery and care-worn "freedom," was of course effective, seen merely as a debater's strategy. It invaded the enemy's camp. Instead of defending it attacked. Instead of relying upon scriptural or other historical testimony, or upon racial theories, the chattel slavery–wage slavery comparison as developed by Fitzhugh addressed the contemporary scene. Indeed it spoke to the world of the future, challenging the bases of large-scale industry. It asked why the philanthropists of the North and of Great Britain ignored the spreading evils of their own societies, concentrating instead upon the alleged horrors of plantation slavery. It drew upon evidence of hardship in Britain, or in cities like New York, and even upon the admissions of people willing to admit their previous ideas about the South were wrong. Fitzhugh, for instance, could refer to a "Mr. Lester, a New York abolitionist," who "after a long and careful . . . study of the present condition of the English laboring class, solemnly avers . . . that he would sooner subject his child to Southern slavery, than have him to be a free laborer of England."[3] And, as expounded by Fitzhugh, the analysis led to an arresting conclusion. Labor had always entailed a kind of servitude; laborers were manifestly inferior to their employers. Modern production techniques necessitated a submissive work force, yet were so harsh in their effect upon the workers that they jeopardized social harmony. The proper organization of the work force was a task of immense and alarming urgency for the modern world. The South had solved the problem by means of plantation slavery, which was both precapitalist and post-capitalist. The South had set the pattern for others to imitate.

This is not the occasion to delve into the philosophy of George Fitzhugh. Certainly he pushed his argument to extremes. Perhaps he had to, in following up his own premises. At any rate, he saw the weakness in the tactic of criticizing British or Northern industrial poverty, if the intention were simply to show Southern slavery in a better light. If "white slavery" was deplorable, how could such a disclosure be used to support the contention that chattel or "black" slavery was a positive good? Whatever the inner logic of Fitzhugh's theorems, their profound and disquieting implications may have tempted his readers to dismiss him as an isolated and eccentric figure. Some commentaries try to rule him out as a cranky rural lawyer-journalist, dreaming up brilliant yet fatally flawed blueprints like the misguided enthusiasts who

keep thinking they have discovered the secret of perpetual motion.[4]

Fitzhugh was in some ways impishly perverse. He
took the argument for slavery further than most, as
Eugene Genovese rather admiringly maintains, and
managed to annoy a number of Southern writers who
felt he was a reckless generalizer.[5] It is true that Fitzhugh was not a systematic, cautious scholar. As he admitted, his information and ideas were often picked up
miscellaneously from periodicals. Historians may therefore disagree as to his importance among apologists for
slavery. For our purposes, however, the salient point
about George Fitzhugh is that he was not an isolated
figure, shut off from the cogitations of the world outside. The magazines he read in his Port Royal study,
many of them meaty British quarterlies, kept him in
close touch with the authors and theories of the day. In
essence, Fitzhugh enlarged upon assumptions that had
already become current on both sides of the Atlantic.
He extrapolated from the writings of a long line of Europeans and Americans who, for a variety of reasons,
had pondered the connections between chattel slavery
and other forms of labor. Fitzhugh, and Grayson, were
thus far from unusual in their formulation of the basic
terms of the debate. By the 1850s, these terms, if not the
conclusions to be drawn from them, were almost com-
monplaces, a standard repertoire.

Even before the end of the eighteenth century, British writers were perturbed by the harsh conditions im-

posed on laboring families. "Are such things done on Albion's shore?" In *Songs of Innocence and Experience*, published in the 1790s, William Blake expressed his horror at the use of children as chimney sweeps. During the protracted controversy over slavery in the British West Indies, which finally led in 1833 to compensated emancipation, spokesmen on both sides frequently compared the lot of plantation slaves to that of the labor force in Britain.[6] Allusions to "wage" or "white" slavery were commonplace in the South long before 1850. As early as 1814, Thomas Jefferson consoled himself by reflecting that Southern slaves lived without fear of destitution, "a solace which few laborers of England possess." John Randolph of Roanoke, traveling in England and Ireland with his black manservant Johnny, wrote to a friend back home: "Much as I was prepared to see misery in the South of Ireland, I was utterly shocked at the condition of the poor peasantry between Limerick and Dublin. Why, sir, John never felt so proud of being a *Virginia slave*. He looked with horror upon the mud hovels and miserable food of the *white slaves*, and I had no fear of his running away." In the Virginia legislature's remarkably candid emancipation debates of January 1832, the opponents as well as the supporters of chattel slavery accepted the proposition that the average Southern slave was, in material comfort, at least on a par with the average European worker. Fitzhugh's reasoning on the necessity for slavery was anticipated by John Randolph, and elsewhere—for example, by the author of a long letter to the *Southern Literary Messenger* in 1843:

One portion of the community always has, and always will live upon the labor of the other portion. In this respect, therefore, the African slave and the European operative stand upon a common platform. . . . The only question with the operative is—what *form* his slavery shall assume? Shall he be the slave of a *master,* whose interest will nurture him in infancy, and whose humanity will provide for him in old age; or shall he be the slave of the *community,* which . . . bequeaths to him, in the decline of his days, as a remuneration for a life of . . . unremitting toil, . . . the happy alternative of starvation, or the parish [i.e., public charity]? . . . Which entails the least suffering upon its victim? This, disguise it as you may, is the true question! Let the *actual present condition* of the African race in the Southern States of the Union and that of the agricultural and commercial operatives of England answer it.[7]

And of course John C. Calhoun was well known for his contention that the entrepreneurs of the North shared with Southern planters the root problem of how to reconcile their workers to their station in life.

Though more imaginative than his fellows, Fitzhugh was not, then, the inventor of utterly outlandish analyses. His writings, which circulated quite widely in the United States, were in fair accord with the views of several predecessors and contemporaries.[8] And they drew upon a mass of Anglo-American deliberation which sought to expose, to reform, or at least to make sense of the social and economic trends of the time.

Our inquiry thus places the antebellum South in the wider context of what has been dubbed the "Atlantic civilization." These are the questions to be considered first. How, where, and when did the concept of "wage" or "white" slavery become prominent in the Anglo-American literature? Did workingmen in Britain and the United States think of themselves as "wage slaves"? How did the concept impinge upon the Anglo-American antislavery campaign mounted by William Lloyd Garrison and other abolitionists in the 1830s? What of the abolitionists themselves: how did they handle the comparison, so frequently drawn, between chattel and wage slavery? And did their attitudes differ fundamentally from those of their many critics? The answers to these questions remain complicated, though recent scholarship, in the course of revising older interpretations, offers fascinating insights. Yet this very complexity is a key to understanding. To gain a genuine sense of the hopes, fears, and predicaments of antebellum America, we must be aware of transatlantic elements. We must recognize too that socioeconomic issues refused to divide neatly, so to speak, into black and white. Nor into pro- and antislavery; nor into clearcut alignments of North and South.

In the Anglo-American heritage, the enjoyment of rights to life, liberty, and property was much insisted upon. The opposite of "liberty" was "slavery." Eighteenth-century Englishmen, singing the popular patriotic song "Rule Britannia," insisted that so long as Britain ruled the waves, she would never have to waive the rules safeguarding personal freedom. With a strong navy to shelter them, "Britons never, never, never will be slaves." The American colonists, in the protests that reached a climax with the Declaration of Independence, constantly complained that the royal government was attempting to treat them as "slaves." The associations of the word, among white Anglo-Americans, were, it is obvious, powerfully emotive and pejorative.

This in part explains why the word was invoked in 1830 by Richard Oastler, a good-hearted Wesleyan Methodist from the North of England, in a series of letters to a Leeds newspaper on "Yorkshire Slavery." Oastler himself at that period had a comfortable post as agent of a Yorkshire country estate. He was keenly involved in the current movement to abolish slavery in the West Indies. Oastler was shocked to hear from a friend, a Yorkshire textile ·manufacturer named John Wood, that small children in the Bradford woollen mills were kept at work from six in the morning until seven at night. Wood was a relatively kind employer. He allowed his child-laborers forty minutes for lunch; in the town's other factories the children had only a half-hour break. Their meager wages were reduced if they came late. They were liable to be beaten by overseers for falling asleep or for making mistakes.

Oastler's friend remarked on the inconsistency of people of their stamp. Church-going, attached to temperance and good causes in general, they seemed blind to what was happening under their noses. Some modest efforts had been made to improve conditions for children employed in the cotton mills of Lancashire. Why the delay in realizing that the same miseries existed even nearer home, across the Pennines in the Yorkshire woollen industry?

Once Oastler was aroused he swung into action. As pamphleteer, platform orator, and member of Parliament, he was to devote the rest of his life to improving the situation of the factory hand, for instance, through a crusade for a ten-hour working day. In his first "Yorkshire Slavery" letter, published in October 1830, Oastler made explicit the irony that, while Yorkshire clergy and Yorkshire's representatives in the House of Commons were castigating the West Indian sugar planters, in their own county "thousands of our fellow-creatures . . . are this very moment . . . in a state of slavery, *more horrid* than are the victims of that hellish system *'colonial slavery.'*" He underlined the analogy: "The blacks may fairly be compared to beasts of burden, *kept for their master's use*; the whites, to those *which others keep and let for hire.*"

Some indignant manufacturers challenged Oastler's facts or his grasp of economic reality, or deplored his extreme language. The workmen and their sympathizers were delighted. Oastler was thanked at a public dinner for speaking out on behalf of "white slaves, both male and female, young and old, in England." A mass meeting in another Yorkshire town voted to congratulate "Richard Oastler Esq. for his . . . manly letters to expose the conduct of those pretended philanthropists and canting hypocrites who travel to the West Indies in search of slavery, forgetting that there is a more abominable and degrading system of slavery at home."[9] Here, then, in England in 1830 we have a conspicuous example of the popularization of the interchangeable terms *wage slavery* and *white slavery*. We note also the seeming

readiness of textile workers to accept instead of scornfully repudiating the claim that they too were slaves—
and possibly worse off than chattel slaves in the New
World.

As we have seen, the comparison did not originate
with Oastler. But it seems to have acquired a new promi-
nence and sharpness from about 1830 onward. Thus
Michael Sadler, a fellow-Yorkshireman and friend of
Oastler's, and the author of detailed studies of pauperism, said in an 1832 speech in Parliament that England's
workers were "white slaves." One of the books in Oastler's library was a poem by a Lancashire artisan, written
in the mid-1830s, *The White Slave's Complaint; or, The
Horrors of Cotton Factories.*[10] Several reasons for the
spread of this terminology in Britain may be suggested.
One is the energetic and resourceful propaganda of
men like Oastler and Sadler, themselves deeply stirred,
who were also quick to perceive the shock-value of ex-
pressions such as "white slavery." Among other factors
were the awesomely rapid pace of industrialization,
which seemed overnight to be transforming the actual
and metaphorical landscape; and the determination of
labor leaders to secure improvement, whether through
trade unionism, the Chartist program of constitutional
reform, or enthusiasm for early forms of socialism. The
slavery comparison, whether meant literally or figura-
tively, became a standard feature of reformist and radical analysis. The French theorist Lamennais argued in
his *De l'esclavage moderne* (1839) that the modern prole-
tarian was fundamentally as much in bondage as the

ancient slave or medieval serf. Lamennais was echoed by
the Italian nationalist, Giuseppe Mazzini: "The workman has no freedom of contract: he is a slave: he has no
alternative but hunger or the pay . . . that his employer
offers him." Identical assumptions were made by the
British Chartist Bronterre O'Brien. In 1849 O'Brien
published the first section of a projected full-length
work to be called *The Rise, Progress and Phases of Human
Slavery*. Apparently unaware of the *Communist Manifesto*,
which had not yet been translated into English, O'Brien
like Karl Marx stressed the parallel between the old
structure of chattel slavery and the newer wage slavery
equivalent. In O'Brien's words: "What are called the
'Working Classes' are the slave populations of civilized
countries."[11]

A further possible explanation for the spread of the
concept among British workingmen was annoyance at
the absorption of Parliamentary reformers in West Indian emancipation (taxing Britons in the process, to
compensate the planters), to the neglect of domestic
reform. At any rate, it is clear that Southern pamphle-
teers who alluded to the chattel slavery–wage slavery
comparison were making use of material already established across the Atlantic, even though their motives
were in general very different.

Indeed, Americans North and South could and did
pay heed to a mass of British self-criticism. They drew
upon the many and substantial articles in important
periodicals like the *Edinburgh Review* and the *Westminster
Review*, often quoting verbatim from them. They were

familiar with the London *Times*, a no less influential source that printed long editorials on the sufferings of the poor. Through such media they followed the discussion in Britain of a host of serious problems, including the application of the new Poor Law of 1834, which thrust the unemployed into dehumanized workhouses, and the unrest of British workingmen, expressing itself by stages in machine-breaking riots, in lockouts and mass meetings, and in emigration overseas.

Americans studied the exposés of a succession of Parliamentary commissions, on the wages, housing, and health of workers not only in the textile mills but in the coalmines, the potteries, the garment trade, and other industries, together with the conditions of life for agricultural workers. Such reports, heavily relied upon also by Friedrich Engels for his *Condition of the English Working Class in 1844*, revealed the price paid for economic growth in low wages, bad food, disease, illiteracy, and immorality. True, this voluminous evidence led, as intended, to reforms, and by the 1850s to a less grim spirit. But until then the combination of injustice and protest, augmented by many signs of discontent in continental Europe, induced apprehension that violent revolution was an equally likely outcome.

Misery barely mitigated: such was the message gleaned by Americans from, for instance, the radically conservative essays of Thomas Carlyle (*Chartism*, 1839; *Past and Present*, 1843; *Latter-Day Pamphlets*, 1850), which stimulated readers as different as Fitzhugh and Ralph Waldo Emerson.[12] American publishers evidently believed there was a market for more modest, factual descriptions. An anonymous book by an Englishman, *The Laboring Classes of England*, published in Boston in 1847, went into a second edition the following year.[13]

Those who preferred to glean their impressions from fiction again had an abundance of material. Charles Dickens was the prime Anglo-American favorite, blending entertainment and humanitarian indignation in his *Oliver Twist* (1837–39), *Nicholas Nickleby* (1838–39), *Hard Times* (1854), and other novels. The Tory Democracy of Benjamin Disraeli was elegantly yet earnestly conveyed in novels like *Coningsby, or The New Generation* (1844), *Sybil, or The Two Nations* (1845), and *Tancred, or The New Crusade* (1847), whose sober subtitles remind us that in each Disraeli felt he had a lesson to impart as well as a romance to narrate. Among other well-known novels, also furnished with socially conscious titles, were Mrs. Frances Trollope's *The Life and Adventures of Michael Armstrong, the Factory Boy* (1839–40),[14] Mrs. Elizabeth Gaskell's *Mary Barton, A Tale of Manchester Life* (written 1845–47), and Charles Kingsley's *Alton Locke, Tailor and Poet* (1850). In poetry there was the much-quoted "Song of the Shirt," by Thomas Hood, first published in the Christmas number of *Punch* (1843), and reprinted in full by Fitzhugh in *Cannibals All!*, he in turn borrowing from an article in the *Edinburgh Review* of January 1849.[15]

The "condition of England," in short, was a topic so omnipresent that Americans could hardly have avoided it even if they had wished to. The terrible disaster of the

Irish potato famine in the 1840s alerted them to other evils in the British Isles. They could read too of the sharp deterioration in the economy of the British West Indies after emancipation, and of the wrongs of British imperial rule in India and elsewhere—colonies in which living standards were said to be abysmally low.

Not every contributor to this immense and somber literature explicitly described the artisans of Britain, or of the Empire, as slaves. Some did, however, and those who did not nevertheless appeared to affirm that the word was not altogether inappropriate to denote such dismal circumstances. This is the background to the adoption of the comparison by writers inside the United States.

But before examining the American scene we must look further at the reactions of British workingmen. Their attitudes were various and altered with the passage of time. Broadly speaking, they resented the preoccupation of the privileged classes with issues far from home. They were susceptible to the argument that, at least on the plantations of the American South, black slave families were relatively well cared for; and, after the end of slavery in Jamaica and other West Indian islands, the American South naturally became the focus for chattel–wage slavery comparisons. British workmen tended to maintain that their own freedom was somewhat illusory. Few could vote in parliamentary elections. Few owned their homes; in the worst slums whole families were crowded into one room. They had no pensions, little or no savings, little or no chance of moving to another employment, another district, or another country unless they were still young, single, and exceptionally lucky. The more militant among them, while hostile to the Tory landed aristocracy and the established Church, were also suspicious of the rising Whig commercial and manufacturing interest. The militants were not converted to the campaign of the 1840s against the protective agricultural tariff known as the Corn Laws. Free Trade, the doctrine of the anti–Corn Law Whigs, who secured repeal of the Laws in 1846, was seen by class-conscious labor spokesmen in Britain as the triumph of capitalism, with its ruthless rationale of profit and loss.

Like William Grayson and other Southern proslavery authors, therefore, they attacked the philanthropists of "Exeter Hall," the London headquarters of reformism, opened in 1831.[16] They heard that Prince Albert, the husband of Queen Victoria, was sympathetic to abolitionism, and knew that the Queen's uncle, the Duke of Sussex, presided over the closing session of the grandly named World's Anti-Slavery Convention in London in 1840. William Lloyd Garrison, one of several American delegates who attended the convention, subsequently traveled north into Scotland to speak at antislavery rallies. At the door of one meeting, in Glasgow, Garrison was handed a leaflet headed *"Have We No White Slaves?"* The author, one Charles M'Ewan, was identified by Garrison as "probably . . . a Chartist or Socialist." His leaflet, which Garrison manfully read aloud to the meeting, contained a bitter criticism of British abolitionists. Garrison, insisting that the "operatives and laborers of

Great Britain and Ireland" were not in any meaningful sense "slaves," appealed to the audience to tell him whether British abolitionists were not already "the best friends of suffering humanity at home." Perhaps to his surprise, he was greeted with shouts of "No! no! no!" Not satisfied by Garrison's response at the meeting, M'Ewan sent a long letter to Garrison's magazine *The Liberator*. In the letter, which Garrison duly printed, M'Ewan expressed intense annoyance that Garrison's main recommendation to the British workman was to reform himself, above all by abstaining from alcohol. "Our argument here," M'Ewan retorted,

is not about minor points; . . . we admit the want of virtue to some extent, but the question with us is—Have we rights to address, and wrongs to complain of? Does justice reign supreme, and the bounties of a kind Providence crown the efforts of the virtuous with impartial hand? No. A bloated Aristocracy, supported by your admirers, and the minions of a lawless faction, have gorged upon the life-springs of the indigent, until penury has filled the land with paupers, crime and degradation; our political horizon is daily darkening; . . . the poor man's fireside is hourly becoming a scene of desolation, and yet your sapient lovers of freedom look coolly on, with perfect indifference to the claims of suffering humanity.[17]

Another Scottish artisan, a weaver named William Thomson who had spent some time in the American South, published a book in 1842 which asserted that British "slavery" was worse than what he had witnessed in the United States.[18]

Moreover, there were special reasons in Scotland for objecting to the opinions of Harriet Beecher Stowe, author of the phenomenally popular *Uncle Tom's Cabin* (1852), over a million copies of which are said to have been sold in Britain within a short period. During the course of a triumphal tour of Britain in 1853, Mrs. Stowe was made welcome in the homes of the great and famous. One of her most cordial hostesses was the Duchess of Sutherland, who was not only a celebrity among philanthropists but among the richest land-owners in Scotland. In Scotland the Duchess's family was accused of having heartlessly dispossessed hundreds of Highland crofters. In a travel account, published on her return to America, Harriet Beecher Stowe gave high praise to the Sutherlands for their enlightened land policies, though at that stage she had not actually seen their Highland estates. Infuriated Scots denounced her. "Mrs. Stowe (the wretch)" is the inscription, in a con-temporary hand, at the front of a copy of the first edi-tion of *Uncle Tom's Cabin* held by Edinburgh's University Library. *Reynolds's Newspaper*, a London radical publica-tion, reacted to Mrs. Stowe's visit with an attack on the Sutherlands and on other well-connected British "pseudo-philanthropists." It was, said *Reynolds's*, "the most miserable affectation or else a downright impos-ture for any *clique* of exclusives . . . to send forth their ranting, canting nonsense, under the guise of sympathy, across the Atlantic, when they have no compassion for the wage-slavery that enchains millions of our people at home."[19]

British workingmen were of course, unlike Fitzhugh, concerned not to extend or justify slavery but to emphasize their own grievances. They were not proslavery. From time to time groups of them lent support to antislavery manifestoes. During the American Civil War they were to be placed on record as endorsing the Union cause. But recent scholarship has considerably modified the notion that while the British aristocracy leaned to the Confederacy, the lower classes were staunchly committed to emancipation and to Union victory. In truth, many remained suspicious of American conduct, and continued to accuse antislavery leaders of hypocrisy. Such skepticism was to be found among the old Chartist and radical activists, some of whom visited or even settled in the United States, and also among younger representatives of the British working class.[20]

When we turn to the United States, the story is remarkably similar. Again, workingmen (or those who spoke on their behalf) were naturally enough not in favor of slavery in the abstract. In the 1850s some labor groups became vocal in their opposition to the extension of chattel slavery in the Territories. The newly formed Republican party sought their votes by appealing to the fear that slavery might become universal in the United States.

As in Britain, however, there seems to have been a reluctance on the part of labor and radical movements of whatever persuasion to denounce the slaveholding South. Those who simply responded to the emotive connotation of the word *slave* applied it to their own circumstances, in a bid for attention.[21] Those who attempted a more elaborate economic analysis were apt to agree with European theories that laborers were people held to servitude, and that the concentration of capital was leading inexorably to the degradation of the worker.

One of the most powerful of such statements, nominally a review of Thomas Carlyle's *Chartism*, was an essay by Orestes Brownson on "The Laboring Classes" (1840). Brownson was at that time an ardent Democrat, on the party's radical wing. There were, he wrote, two systems of labor, slave and free.

Of the two, the first is, . . . except so far as the feelings are concerned, decidedly the least oppressive. . . . As to actual freedom, one has just about as much as the other. The laborer at wages has all the disadvantages of freedom and none of its blessings, while the slave, if denied the blessings, is freed from the disadvantages. We are no advocates of slavery; . . . but we say frankly that, if there must always be a laboring population distinct from proprietors and employers, we regard the slave system as decidedly preferable to the system of wages.

Brownson, writing in a period of economic depression, described the growing plight of the American artisan, male and female. Alluding to the 1840 presidential campaign, he derided the rich, selfish, Northern Whig who "shouts for liberty, stickles for equality, and is horrified at a Southern planter who keeps slaves." It was cheaper, said Brownson, for the Northern employer to hire labor. "Wages is a cunning device of the devil, for the benefit of tender consciences, who would retain all the advantages of the slave system without the expense, trouble, and odium of being slaveholders." Given the tendencies of the modern world, emancipation was futile; it would leave the Southern black "a slave still, though with the title and cares of a freeman." Brownson's remedy, somewhat vaguely framed, was a total reconstruction of the economic order.[22]

Brownson can be diagnosed as an intellectually fickle eccentric. It is true that not long after the Whig victory of 1840 he abandoned his radical principles. He entered the Catholic church; and by the early 1850s shifted so far as to be lecturing Southern students (in Maryland) on the organic virtues of chattel slavery. Yet one can sense a certain permeability or porosity between "radical" and "conservative" views where the equivocal theme of slavery was concerned. As Fitzhugh could imaginatively comprehend socialism, so Brownson could imaginatively encompass conservatism: conservatism, that is, as a desire for an equilibrium in society. Both, after all, were in quest of social harmony; and, in common with many of their American contemporaries, neither was quite sure whether "liberty" was the feasible or even desirable antithesis of "slavery."[23]

Yet we do not need to produce elaborate explanations for Brownson, any more than for Fitzhugh. We can find plenty of other Northern testimony couched in the same terms as those of Brownson's essay. In 1832 Seth Luther, a New England labor spokesman, claimed to have seen at first hand that slave children were happier than "the white children . . . in the cotton mills in free New England." The parallel was drawn again and again. In

1844 the shoemakers of Lynn, Massachusetts, declared: "We are slaves in the strictest sense of the word. For do we not have to toil from the rising of the sun to the going down of the same for our masters—aye, masters, and for our daily bread?"[24]

These were more or less the views of native-born Americans, as expressed for example in the *National Trades Union*, the publication of the union organization of that name. They seem to have been the views too of the majority of English and Scottish immigrants. Irish immigrant workmen were notoriously uninvolved in American radical controversies, including the slavery issue. German immigrants, according to legend, were more politically conscious. But even those such as Wilhelm Weitling who were early converts to communism appear either to have avoided the antislavery movement, or to have confined themselves to the assertion that they were opposed to *all* forms of slavery.[25]

This indifference can be accounted for in various ways. One is that American white workers, like those in Britain, understandably gave priority to their own problems. Another is that they feared the competition they would face from free black labor.[26] A third explanation is sheer racial prejudice, an attitude manifested, for instance, in *Negro-Mania* (1851), a vehemently anti-black compendium by a Philadelphia typesetter named John Campbell. A fourth factor is the tendency of workingmen, before the realignment of national politics in the 1850s, to attach themselves as Brownson had done to the Democratic party. They saw the Democrats as more sympathetic to labor than the Whig party; yet the Democrats were also more attuned to the white Southern viewpoint. Whatever relative weight we give to these or other factors, even radical historians have not been able to show convincingly that the antebellum labor movement in the United States had much sympathy with the antislavery campaign.

The same is true of the reformist doctrines of Robert Owen, Fourier, and other Europeans, disseminated in the United States through the activities of Albert Brisbane and the New York newspaper editor Horace Greeley. The main remedy of these pro-labor utopians was land reform, whether to be worked communally, as in the Owenite model, or in the redistributed individual farm units advocated by the "Associationists." In the words of one Associationist editorial:

A reform in the institution of Slavery . . . must proceed hand in hand with a great and radical Social Reform, and chattel slavery like all other kinds of servitude, should be extinguished gradually as the false relations . . . connected with Industry, which originate and maintain it, are corrected and abolished. . . .

The primary cause of Slavery is repugnant and dishonorable industry. So long as Labor is allowed to remain in its present . . . degrading and ill-requited condition, slavery and servitude under various forms will continue to exist. We must go to the roots of the Evil; we must extirpate the cause before we attempt to destroy the effect.[27]

Another American, lecturing on Associationist principles, was reported as saying that slavery in the South "was only one of many forms of slavery that existed on the earth. . . . Consequently they did not contemplate the removal of this one evil alone; . . . they wished to abolish all . . . forms of slavery. They considered the White Slavery of the North in many respects worse than the Black Slavery of the South. It was more heartless and had less direct sympathy with its victims." The free white laborers of the North, according to the lecturer, were doomed to fall into a wage slavery as harsh as that of Europe, unless wholesale social reforms were carried out.[28]

A more fully reasoned discussion of slavery, in its various contexts, was supplied by Horace Greeley, in declining an invitation to attend an antislavery convention in Cincinnati. For Greeley, "wherever . . . the relation between the servant and the served is not one of affection and reciprocal good offices, but of authority, social ascendancy and power over subsistence on the one hand, and of necessity, servility and degradation on the other—there, in my view, is Slavery." Hence, Greeley said, "If I am less troubled concerning the Slavery prevalent in Charleston or New-Orleans, it is because I see so much Slavery in New-York, which appears to claim my first efforts . . . how can I devote myself to a crusade against distant servitude, when I discern its essence pervading my own immediate community? nay, when I have not yet succeeded in banishing it from my own humble household?"[29]

Underlying such judicious utterances was a disapproval of abolitionists sometimes amounting to hatred.

The reaction went far beyond the belief that the abolitionists were tactically unwise to focus upon chattel slavery. Labor writers accused the abolitionists of religious fanaticism, of moral complacency, and of callous disregard for the Northern wage slave. An extreme example of vituperation was a pamphlet published in New York in 1850 by H. F. James, a workingman. The title indicates the tone: *Abolitionism Unveiled! Hypocricy Unmasked! and Knavery Scourged! Luminously Portraying the Formal Hocusses, Whining Philanthropists, Moral Coquets, Practical Atheists, and the Hollow-Hearted Swindlers of Labor Yclept the 'Northern Abolitionists.'*[30] Here is another piece of angry rhetoric, from the Philadelphia artisan John Campbell, referring to the struggle in the United States for a shortened working day: "The howls of fanatics . . . as to the sufferings of the southern slaves, and the cruelty of their masters, humanitarianism, rights of man, woman's rights, Negroism, &c., are eternally upon the lips of the abolitionists; but do they sympathize with the white laborer?" Campbell refused to believe that "the New York or New England abolitionists have ever . . . attempted to accomplish anything for their white brethren. Pennsylvania has a ten hour law, New Jersey has another, but no thanks to the abolitionists. The fact is, that some of the bitterest opponents of the ten hour system are rank, rabid abolitionists."[31]

Hostility to the abolitionists, on all sorts of grounds, was widespread among Americans who were not workmen. To some extent they duplicated the objections we have already instanced, though as might be expected they were less concerned with the chattel–wage slavery comparison. Without going into their criticisms at this stage, it can be said that they too charged the abolitionists with foolish and inflammatory agitation.[32]

Were such accusations unjust? On the one hand, Garrison and his fellow abolitionists at the extreme end of the antislavery spectrum were conscious of working-class disapproval, and eager to win at least tacit support. Some abolitionists, such as the Tappan brothers, possessed wealth. But whatever psychic income they may have derived from joining the movement, they certainly did not benefit financially; they used their money to promote abolitionism. The columns of *The Liberator* were opened to workingmen's, as to others', critiques of abolitionism. Of Garrison's colleagues, Wendell Phillips sincerely tried to grapple with the wage slavery issue, and he was later to become an active labor sympathizer. One prominent abolitionist, John A. Collins, took the matter so seriously that he quit the movement and transferred his reforming zeal to collectivism—until he also grew disenchanted with that brand of reform.[33]

Moreover, if slavery in general were evil, and if chattel slavery were arguably the most ominous form, then the abolitionists had a good case for attacking the problem on this particular front. True, they paid little heed to the deplorable treatment of free blacks in the North. Yet they could feel that their campaign for immediate emancipation was more realistic and less hypocritical than the gradualist, recolonizing schemes their movement managed to supplant. Reform must begin *some-*

where: why not tackle a specific, definable wrong? Most reform movements heighten their effect by focussing upon a single, easily grasped, dramatic aim; and also by vivid, even garish depictions of the wrong they wish to right. In this respect, perhaps the abolitionists could not afford to concede that plantation slavery might be in its own terms a humane institution, or that so-called free enterprise might leave workers distinctly unfree. To admit such disquieting evidence would have robbed abolitionism of its force, just as temperance advocates would have failed to gain the ear of the American public if they had pictured careers and homes that were *not* ruined by alcohol. The abolitionist difficulty was greater, indeed: their crusade would have been altered out of all recognition if they had endeavored to direct a dual assault, on both chattel slavery and wage slavery.

A deliberate tactical decision to narrow the focus to the single issue of chattel slavery is one thing. More serious, however, is the charge that the abolitionists were fatally incapable of perceiving the actual problems of their time. As some historians have suggested, the abolitionists can be seen as deeply imbued with the competitive or capitalist ethic.[34] Here, of course, the allegation is not that they were fanatics, outside the mainstream of American thought, but that on the contrary they were too much in the mainstream. Translated into moral propositions, such an ethic did, as Brownson and the Associationists claimed, assume that progress depended upon the self-regenerating efforts of the individual. Indeed one abolitionist justification for intervening on behalf of black slaves was that they, and they only, lacked the means to improve their situation. Workingmen were offended, and sometimes infuriated, by being told of their duty to succeed by dint of industry and self-denial. How dare the prosperous classes reprove the poorer ones for indulging in drink or tobacco? What other solace had the poor? In this interpretation, their impoverishment (or immiseration, in the Marxist term) was confronted with nothing more than commiseration, and even that in small doses mingled with injunctions to be worthy of their hire.

It may be that the abolitionists, as critics of at least a part of the American status quo, did conceal a perplexed uneasiness over the emerging industrial order. From time to time, as in an exchange of letters in *The Liberator* in 1847, they did make an effort to come to grips with the proposition that Northern "liberty" was by no means the antithesis of Southern "slavery." It may be that they displaced their uneasiness, however unwittingly, by finding a scapegoat in plantation slavery—a phenomenon far removed in space from the tenements of New York and Boston, the tall chimneys and clanking machinery of modern times.

Yet, as Ronald G. Walters shows in *The Antislavery Appeal*, the majority of abolitionists, like the majority of their countrymen, readily persuaded themselves that technology would be not an enslaving but a liberating feature. Walters reveals that several of them began as enthusiasts for business and technology. As a young man the abolitionist poet John G. Whittier had edited a magazine entitled *The American Manufacturer*. Three years before launching *The Liberator*, William Lloyd Garrison, a keen supporter of Henry Clay's "American System," wrote: "We wish to see a manufactory by the side of every suitable stream." They exulted in the spread of railroads. The conventional wisdom of *laissez-faire* enterprise held that a "free" economic structure was necessarily superior to a restricted one. The slave economy could not possibly prosper—even where the apparent evidence indicated the contrary. A free industrialized economy would not only guarantee prosperity, it would put an end to the drudgery that was held to be synonymous with slavery. So one antislavery crusader predicted that machines "will at last set free a large portion of leisure time from slavery to the elements." Another claimed that the steam engine was destined to be "our artificial slave."[35] The American worker's positive incentive, in the eyes of abolitionists and of many who thoroughly disapproved of their "immediatist" aims, was his capacity to share in the wealth to be generated by the growth of agriculture and industry. The Boston manufacturer Nathan Appleton wrote in 1844: "The high reward of labor in all its branches is the great, the important distinction which diffuses comfort, intelligence and self-respect through the whole mass of the community, in a degree unknown in the previous history of civilization." Here Appleton was in close accord with the Boston abolitionist Wendell Phillips, who in 1847 declared: "I believe the terms 'wages slavery' and 'white slavery' would be utterly unintelligible to an audience of laboring people, as applied to themselves. . . . Does legislation bear hard upon them?—their votes can alter it. Does capital wrong them?—economy will make them capitalists."

The Appletons and the Phillipses shared too a belief in the less genial corollary that competition and the threat of unemployment must act as a negative incentive. "Freedom," in Phillips's words, was a strenuous, and could be a chilly, concept; "to economy, self-denial, temperance, education, and moral and religious character, the laboring class, and every other class in this country, must owe its elevation and improvement."[36]

In the light of history, we may feel that Southern amateur sociologists such as Fitzhugh, and those in Europe and the United States who sought to analyze the world's major social and economic trends, were wiser than either the abolitionists or the complete defenders of the status quo. Those who refused to admit that there might be wage slaves as well as chattel slaves clung to an individualist faith that was perhaps simultaneously too optimistic and too censoriously strict.

At any rate, a striking feature of the controversy over the definitions of "slavery" is its repetitiveness. It presented a challenge hard to meet, and in general not adequately recognized. Fitzhugh's remedy was obviously not acceptable to most Americans—perhaps not even entirely to himself. Some labor and radical spokesmen offered incisive critiques of another sort. Here again their arguments were resisted or ignored by the nation's leaders of opinion. In these circumstances, strange half-alliances were tentatively struck. So, when Senator James H. Hammond of South Carolina referred in a notorious speech of 1858 to the "mud-sill" of the white and black proletariat, he offended many white laborers; yet he also drew letters of thanks from workingmen for noticing their plight.[37]

The chattel slavery–wage slavery conundrum was not the only problem in the path of the American Republic. But it was prominent, and seemingly intractable. It was like a riddle of classical legend, not to be solved within the American consensus.

One hypothetical way out, resorted to by abolitionists and others, was to claim that American conditions were unique. Wage slavery might be conceded to exist in Europe: almost by definition, it could not exist in the New World, and would never develop there if Americans kept the faith.[38] In the next lecture we shall see how certain Americans insisted that wage slavery was a foreign, and especially a British, vice. That being so, Americans must beware of foreign intrusion. They must draw reassurance from the contrast between the New World's essential freedom and the Old World's essential tyranny. We shall see, though, that while such an explanation brought some comfort, it also increased the confusion already investing our subject.

TWO

Anglo-American Discord and the Definition of Slavery

BRITAIN AND THE UNITED STATES HAD A MULTITUDE OF ties during the antebellum decades; some of these have already been touched upon. There were vital and conspicuous economic links. Most of the manufactures entering American ports were from England. The docks of Liverpool were piled high with bales of American cotton—the very basis of Lancashire's giant textile industry. British banking firms such as the Baring Brothers were intimately involved in American affairs. Thousands of British citizens had invested money in American securities and state and municipal bonds. Each nation was the other's best customer. The Episcopal, Presbyterian, Methodist, Baptist, Quaker and other churches maintained an intimate rapport across the Alantic. Reform movements—pacifism, temperance, antislavery—operated in tandem.[1] Fashions in music, drama, costume, decor, and architecture followed the same trends. British authors, classical and contemporary, supplied the bulk of American reading. Writers like Charles Dickens were lionized when they visited the

United States. Whether or not they were established authors, a profusion of British travelers published accounts of their experiences in the New World.[2] The United States was a promised land for many British radicals and liberals.[3]

In this great traffic there was also a constant flow from America to Britain. Among men of letters, Edgar Allan Poe had gone to school in England. Washington Irving, of recent Scottish immigrant stock, had begun his long immersion in the mother country by working in the family hardware business in Liverpool. James Fenimore Cooper lived in Europe for seven years and wrote a book on England. Ralph Waldo Emerson, having visited Britain in 1833 and 1847, distilled his observation in *English Traits* (1856). Nathaniel Hawthorne was American consul in Liverpool from 1853 to 1857; his book on England was entitled *Our Old Home* (1863). Other Americans—clergymen, scholars, merchants, officials, reformers, journalists—stepped ashore by the boatload to satisfy their curiosity. In part they came as pilgrims, eager to pay homage to Sir Walter Scott's Melrose, Shakespeare's Stratford-on-Avon, or the tombs in Westminster Abbey.[4]

Anglo-American circles, then, acknowledged a common heritage and in some respects a continuing set of mutual interests. In a literal sense, Britain *was* "Our Old Home" for many Americans; and in standard British parlance, citizens of the United States were "our American cousins." At banquets and on ceremonial occasions, the orators of both countries proclaimed that blood was

thicker than water. In 1842, for example, Edward Ev-
erett of Massachusetts, the American minister to Britain, said in a speech: "We are united by . . . strong ties.
The roots of our history run into the soil of England.
Hence came our fathers. . . . For every purpose but that
of political jurisdiction we are one people."[5] Using such
sources, one could assert with fair plausibility that
Anglo-American relations were familial and cordial.

Such an interpretation would, however, be misleading. To the extent that they were parts of one family, as
the orators genially announced, the family history was
full of discord. This should not surprise us. Police records show that most quarrels of the kind that lead to
violence occur between relatives within the same family.
Family metaphors had been used again and again as
rhetorical weapons in the disputes preceding the War of
Independence.[6] At that time the metaphor was usually
generational: old versus young, parent versus offspring.
The American child had metaphorically thrown off pa-
rental control, and after a prolonged set of rows moved
out and married into a different milieu. To Americans,
the family analogy thus implied rightful resistance to
insensitive, in fact tyrannical, behavior, of a kind that
cast doubt on whether the "mother country" had ever
been a true parent. The consequence was a deeply felt
American determination to obliterate the old relationship, to reject all British efforts at tutelage or advice. At
best the "old country" or the "old home" could be conceded to be picturesquely "ancient"—with the corollary
that Shakespeare was a common ancestor, not a British

possession. Often, though, the assumption was that the former parent was wicked (a wicked stepmother?), crabbed, and senile. Walt Whitman's contemptuous term for Britain, and other European monarchies, was "moth-eaten."[7] The new world of the United States was by contrast envisaged as youthful, free-spirited, and innovative. For the British, the parent-child metaphor was of course interpreted differently. The parent embodied wisdom, dignity, stability: the child—brash, ungrateful, associating with bad company—must come to a bad end.

The idea of "cousinage," more often referred to in Britain than in America, suggests a modification of the family metaphor: a shift from a generational to a contemporaneous relationship. Perhaps it revealed a recognition, however grudging, that by midcentury the United States was no longer a child, nor a member of the immediate family. By 1850, emerging from the Mexican War and the Oregon settlement, America was clearly a phenomenon to be reckoned with—about on a par with Britain in population, economic promise, and expansionist energy. Yet the metaphor still hinted at a right and a duty to criticize. "Cousinship" may suggest a branch of the family for which one is not to blame, but which is in itself blameworthy. These are the cousins one disapproves of, gossips about, sermonizes over, and perhaps secretly envies.

To speak of Britain and America as a mutual admiration society is to gloss over profound antipathies. But it is not accurate to portray them, alternatively, as nothing but a mutual recrimination society. Each was in itself

richly complex, yet the two had much in common, including an emulative rivalry that served to divide them.
Great Britain was several countries, the heart of a widespread empire. England was traditional, monarchical,
and aristocratic. On the other hand it was the world's
leading industrial, trading, and maritime nation, for-
midably confident of its supremacy over all other lands.
Moreover, the British regarded themselves as the champion of liberal causes in the world: the foes of slavery
and of the Atlantic slave trade, the friends of independence among subject peoples such as the Greeks. They
viewed the regimes of continental Europe as backward
and oppressive. They were increasingly committed to
the principle of international free trade: a seemingly
progressive creed, calling for the removal of customs
barriers (as had been achieved between the states of the
American Union), and for open competition in world
markets.

The United States was likewise a large and diverse
commonwealth, embracing many viewpoints and hardly
more able to reconcile them than were the British. In
theory, if not always in practice, North and South represented social and economic systems profoundly at vari-
ance. While Northern spokesmen, for instance, usually
advocated a protective tariff, the Southern bloc headed
by John C. Calhoun agreed with the British in opting
for free trade. Fierce Anglo-American rivalries came to
the surface over the Great Exhibition held in London's
Crystal Palace in 1851. American commentators from
the North veered between reluctance to respond to the

British initiative in mounting this ambitious international exposition, and angry resentment at the seeming feebleness of the American display. Some Southerners, however, were wryly and dispassionately amused. The *Richmond Enquirer* declared that "the failure of the United States to make a great show in the World's Fair" was a blessing in disguise. "We too often talk as if we were the only civilized nation on earth. . . . It is time that the conceit was taken out of us." The *Charleston Mercury* concurred that Southerners need not share the Yankee disappointment at seeing their exhibits "sink into merited obscurity when brought forward in untariffed competition with those of other countries."[8]

In short, neither Britain nor the United States was a simple, homogeneous unit. The cartoon figures of lean Uncle Sam and corpulent John Bull were in a way crude substitutes for a complex reality. One should hesitate to take at face value the remarks of individuals in either nation about the other. Even their hostile reactions might mask ambivalent feelings of admiration—just as North and South in the United States covertly respected certain features of one another's civilization.[9]

Nevertheless the familial analogy is illuminating, if we stress two key aspects. The first is a sort of fascinated antagonism, in which each nation remained acutely aware of the other, and extremely sensitive to criticism from the other—the Americans, as the younger society, especially so. The second feature is the way in which citizens of the two nations seemed actually to think in stereotypes, and to express themselves in a deliberately

caricatured symbolic language, as if Uncle Sam and
John Bull were living representative figures that had
walked off the street and flattened themselves into two-
dimensional abstractions. The British and the Americans showed a remarkable readiness to visualize their
societies as being in stark, diametric opposition. This, to
repeat, was not their only mode. Yet even where the
observer, as in Emerson's *English Traits*, recognized the
three-dimensionality of the land in question, the interpretation became also an oblique commentary on his
own country. The British served the Americans as a reference group, and vice versa. Commonly, however, each
served as a negative reference group: a means, that is,
of evoking the desired ideal of one's own society by
describing opposite characteristics in the other.

Observers therefore often generalized with reckless
assurance. Each pretended that the other place was fundamentally in error, and that its own principles were
absolutely sound. Each accused the other of chauvinism,
greed, hypocrisy, and an instability that must ultimately
produce an explosion. And the presumed contrast was
most dramatically expressed as a clash between republicanism and monarchy.

As the British saw matters, in their most hostile accounts, American republicanism entailed strident vul-
garity, abject conformity, demagoguery, corrupt politics, and endemic violence. Its values were superficial.
It treasured quantity rather than quality, and pursued
the "Almighty Dollar" with joyless intensity. Despite
their boasted virtue, the Yankees were also a dishonest

nation. This last complaint acquired new force with the financial slump of the late 1830s, when a number of American states and cities defaulted on their interest payments to investors. The British indictment was summed up in a *Punch* cartoon of 1847, "The Land of Liberty." In the foreground lounges an ungainly Uncle Sammish figure, apparently a slaveholder, in a Panama hat, his belt stuffed with weapons. One of his boots is planted upon a toppled bust of George Washington. Behind him are files of manacled blacks, driven by the overseer's lash. The clouds of smoke from his cheroot frame a series of vignettes—a bloody battle in Mexico, a pair of duelists armed with rifles, a Negro about to be lynched, rioters desecrating the altar of a Catholic church, legislators brawling on the floor of an assembly, and—this scene captioned "Repudiation"—an innocent John Bull whose pocket is being picked by a pious-looking American.[10]

It is true that British travelers sometimes paid tribute to the American gentry, North and South, or were favorably impressed by life on Southern plantations. The geologist Sir Charles Lyell, for instance, wrote: "The Negroes, so far as I have yet seen them, whether in domestic service or on the farms, appear very cheerful and free from care, better fed than a large part of the labouring class of Europe."[11]

But in the main, as *Punch's* anthology of American atrocities makes plain, the existence of chattel slavery in the land of the free was for the British the central anomaly. Variously puzzled, righteous, sarcastic, indignant, they pounced on what was for them an absurd and intolerable contradiction. Apart from the muted comments of witnesses like Lyell, or the generally sympathetic responses of a Harriet Martineau, the great majority of well-known British writers (including Harriet Martineau herself) insisted that plantation slavery was a barbarous anachronism for a nation so proud of its democratic ideals. The evils of slavery were among the chief reproaches in Frances Trollope's *Domestic Manners of the Americans* (1832), and the harshest indictment in Dickens's *American Notes for General Circulation* (1842). British commentators did not all agree as to whether slavery was a separate and exceptional horror, or part and parcel of the whole American scene. The radically inclined Harriet Martineau seemed to feel it was a blot on an otherwise handsome landscape. Writers of the Tory persuasion seemed to believe with the *Punch* artist that slavery was a symptom of a pervasively lawless brutality. This was the view of the novelist Captain Marryat, who described the United States *in toto* as "a miserable failure." By and large it was the opinion also of Mrs. Trollope and of Dickens, leading to the conclusion that Britain and America were antitheses: civilization confronting barbarism.[12]

H. L. Mencken remarks somewhere that what hurts is not injustice, but justice. It may be that some of the British criticisms were justified. They were after all not very different from what Americans said about themselves in less euphoric moments. James Fenimore Cooper, for instance, published caustic comments on the tyranny exercised by the ill-educated majority in his native land, which could almost have been composed by Dickens.[13] Yet much depends in such matters upon who delivers the verdict. The point is nicely made by Carl Degler, in explaining the attitudes of liberally minded Southerners. "For," he notes, "despite the examples of suppression throughout the antebellum years, it was always possible, at least in the upper South, to discuss the disadvantages, if not the outright evil, of slavery," as long as certain conditions were met. "One was that the person making the criticism be a native Southerner—not an outlander or worse, a Northerner."[14] Whether Southerners were more annoyed by Northern or by British condemnations is debatable. What does seem axiomatic is that so-called home truths are not acceptable when they originate from outside the home.

Yet it is apparent that Americans doubly resented castigation from British sources. How dare the condescending visitor from "Our Old Home" presume still to occupy the role of parent or guardian? An additional factor may have been American disappointment that rebukes should come from the very authors they relied upon for home truths about the British scene. Dickens had delighted them as the passionately eloquent delineator of British wrongdoing—a democrat by instinct and so almost an honorary American. Yet his travel book poured scorn upon "Republican America." The nation, he told a friend, was "a body without a head; the arms and legs are occupied in quarreling with the trunk

and with each other, and exchanging bruises at random"—another vignette, so to speak, from the *Punch*
rendering of the "Land of Liberty." America, said Dickens, was "not the Republic of my imagination": give him
a monarchy, at least the British monarchy, any day.[15] In
inverted chronology, Frances Trollope, too, dismayed
and exasperated her American readers. How could the
same author have produced the heartfelt account of
Michael Armstrong, the Factory Boy (1840), and the super-
cilious *Domestic Manners of the Americans* (1832)?

British commentators on the United States did un-
doubtedly tend to assume a tone of well-bred superiority, as if each were actually of noble birth. William
Cobbett, a sturdy radical in Britain, conducted himself
as a crotchety conservative when in the United States:
"Peter Porcupine" was his appropriate American pen-
name. Frances Trollope, who had been brought up in
a middle-class home, was jeered at in the American
press as "Dame Trollope" because she put on the airs
of a *grande dame* in analyzing the unforgivable crudity
of cities such as Cincinnati. Charles Dickens likewise
adopted an oddly baronial literary persona to cover his
American visit. Each of these, perhaps unconsciously,
slipped into the demeanor of a respectable monarchist
confronted by a disreputable republic.

If so, the compliment was repaid in full by the more
pungent American critics of Britain. For them that land
was, exactly as their revolutionary forebears had insisted, a fundamentally undemocratic country. At the

top of the pyramid stood (or reclined) the monarchy, which in American eyes was as expensive as it was superfluous. The royal family was alleged to cost the British taxpayer as much as the entire outlay of the United States government.[16] Even more of a target were the aristocracy, with their hereditary titles and their vast estates. The upper class were thought to be hand in glove with the Church of England, whose bishops held seats in the House of Lords. They all, it was said, battened upon the poor, many of whom were believed to be near destitution.

The portrait was of course not imaginary, even where tinged with prejudice. Americans were often genuinely startled by their first glimpses of British poverty, and scandalized by the disparity between magnificence and misery. Herman Melville's exposure to the slums of Liverpool, where he had arrived as a young sailor, is hauntingly conveyed in his semi-autobiographical novel *Redburn* (1849). Furthermore, as we have seen, Americans could draw upon a substantial British literature of social observation. Some of their own books consisted largely of slabs of quotation interspersed with editorial moralizing. Thus in 1853, John C. Cobden, who seems to have been a Northerner, published a four-hundred-page book called *The White Slaves of England*.[17] He took copious extracts from Parliamentary reports and from articles in periodicals, including Dickens's magazine *Household Words*. He made use of Dickens's *Nicholas Nickleby*, Kingsley's *Alton Locke*, Mrs. Gaskell's *Mary Bar-*

ton, Mrs. Trollope's *Michael Armstrong* (from which his
publisher borrowed the front illustration), and the brilliant word-pictures Henry Mayhew sketched of the
Cockney underworld. Cobden cited other British material on conditions in Ireland, India, and Mauritius, and
on such vicious customs as the impressment of unof-
fending citizens into naval service. The British might
object that in American hands these injustices were dis-
torted by factual errors and by animus, or derived from
old sources whose information was out of date. Cobden,
for example, mentioned Robert Southey's *Letters from
Espriella*, a fictional satire that seemed to intrigue Americans, without noting that it had been published back in
1807.[18]

What probably stung most, though, was the *tu quoque*,
or tit-for-tat assault: the rejoinder to British complaints
against the United States that reversed the particulars
of the charge so as to attribute to the mother country the
basic vices of brutality, hypocrisy, and unstable contradiction. In Cobden's words:

A government originating in, and suited for, a barbarous age
must necessarily be unfit for one enjoying the meridian of
civilization. . . . It is the sin of the English government that it
. . . throws the gloomy shadow of feudalism over some of the
fairest regions of the earth. It legislates for the age of William
the Conqueror instead of the reign of Victoria. The few for
hereditary luxury and dominion, the many for hereditary
misery and slavery, is the grand fundamental principle of the
English system. . . . In no country are the few richer than in
England, and in no country are the masses more fearfully
wretched.

Compare Dickens on America: "I love and honor very many people here, but the 'mass' (to use our monarchial terms) are miserably dependent in great things, and miserably independent in small ones."[19]

A reproof as fierce as Cobden's is to be found in other American works—most of them, we should emphasize, by Northerners. A further example will suffice, from a book by William Dix (1855) arraigning the British for having made alliance in the Crimean War with infidel Turkey against Christian Russia. The author turns aside from his main argument to assert:

The upheaving of England has begun, and it will not be checked until her whole structure has been pervaded by the spirit of reform. An hereditary aristocracy ruling a mighty realm; . . . coronets protecting sin, and miters stained with nepotism; prescription, favoritism, routine, everywhere usurping the place of merit, energy, and strength; wars lost by etiquette—men sacrificed by etiquette—disease, disaster, and ruin, assisted by etiquette—a nation at the point of death by prescription—a throne almost gone, from worship of precedent—a church in danger of spiritual palsy; if such anomalies as these receive not immediate and vigorous correction, the empire of the British Isles may as well fold her wings at once and die upon her funeral pile.[20]

Sometimes, too, Americans discovered themselves maintaining ideas they did not usually hold, when faced with patronizing British comments. James Fenimore Cooper was more of a republican democrat in Europe than in his native habitat. The cultivated, rather haughty American naval officer Alexander Slidell Mackenzie, among

his countrymen—and perhaps especially in the privacy
of the officers' mess—would probably have dismissed
Andrew Jackson as an uneducated boor. But he was so
irritated by the remarks of Englishmen with whom he
shared a coach on the road from London to Brighton,
that he became belatedly converted to "the virtues of the
hickory-tree."[21]

So far, the American criticisms we have alluded to
seem restricted to the iniquities of monarchical, aristocratic, and imperial Britain. How could they accommodate this image with the fact that Britain was also in the
forefront of the Industrial Revolution? How could a
moribund society be so active, on her own ground and
on everyone else's around the world? The answer, of
course, is that they regarded the new Britain as only a
modern extension of the old. The manufacturers of
Manchester, Leeds, or Birmingham, self-made and bus-
tling, apparently quite unlike the arrogant landowners
of the hereditary aristocracy, were, according to Americans, themselves "money barons." There was really
no conflict between the two groups. New wealth reinforced old wealth, and soon mingled with it. Feudal
serfdom modulated into wage slavery or, in extremis,
into pauperism.

Cobden's *White Slaves of England* illustrates the reasoning process. Each successive chapter presents the
various forms of poverty and exploitation in Britain,
Ireland, and the British colonies as linked elements in a
fatal system. There is for him no essential difference between the situation of agricultural laborers in Britain

and that of workers in the mines, foundries, mills, and sweatshops. Without regard to age or sex, all are victimized. By the same token, Britain's soldiers and sailors are unfree. They are signed on for long terms of service (usually twenty-one years in the infantry), and subject to flogging—a degrading punishment which was of course portrayed by abolitionists as one of the worst aspects of plantation slavery. People convicted even of minor crimes such as stealing food, are liable to be transported, sometimes for life, to the penal settlements of Australia. The peasants and coolies of other lands under the British flag are no less the victims of the urge of British landlords and manufacturers for power or profit. The aristocrat finds lucrative posts for his relatives and associates in India; the "money baron" sells his cotton goods there to the detriment of native manufactures.[22]

British depravity, and the notion of an identity of aim between the landed aristocracy and the "Lords of the Loom," are conveyed in "Black and White Slaves," a lithograph published in New York by A. Donnelly in 1844. It consists of two contrasting panels, headed AMERICA and ENGLAND. In the American scene, slaves take their ease on a Southern plantation, watched approvingly by a refined young planter and his family. "God bless you massa!" exclaims an elderly slave, "you feed and clothe us. When we are sick you nurse us and when we are too old for work you provide for us." His master, gazing piously heavenward, reflects: "These poor creatures are a sacred legacy from my ancestors and while a dollar is left me, nothing shall be spared to

Chattel and wage, or "black" and "white," slavery are seen as
A. Donnelly in New York. The scene on the right could
Trollope's novel *Michael Armstrong, the Factory Boy*. It is
the product of a Southern press but was issued in the North
See also Carl Bode, ed., *American Life in the 1840s* (Garden

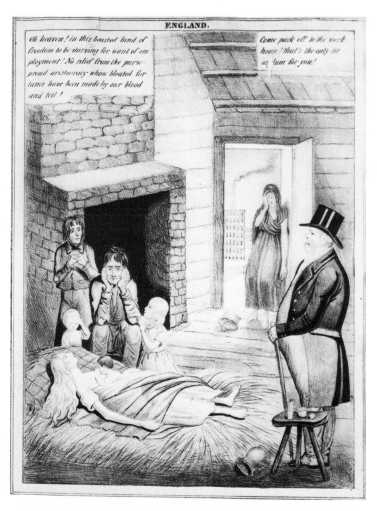

ENGLAND.

Oh heaven! in this boasted land of freedom to be starving for want of em ployment! No relief from the purse-proud aristocracy whose bloated fortunes have been made by our blood and toil!

Come pack off to the work-house! that's the only as lum for you!

dramatic opposites in this caricature of 1844, published by
well have been based on such British accounts as Frances
interesting to note that the idealized plantation scene was not
(presumably in this case by an Irish-American printmaker).
City, N.Y.: Doubleday, 1967), pp. 366–68.

Courtesy of the New-York Historical Society, New York City increase their comfort and happiness." In the ENGLAND panel, on the other hand, a destitute man crouches in a bare hovel before an unlit fire among his ragged children. His wife, perhaps dead of starvation, is a wan figure stretched out upon a bed of straw. Through the open door can be seen a tall factory whose chimney belches smoke. The worker's bitter and despairing words are: "Oh heaven! in this boasted land of freedom to be starving for want of employment! No relief from the purse-proud aristocracy whose bloated fortunes have been made by our blood and toil!" He is answered by a fat, arrogant, top-hatted person, perhaps intended by the caricaturist to be a composite of "purse-proud" aristocrat and greedy manufacturer: "Come pack off to the work house! that's the only fit asylum for you!"

Such too was the implicit indictment of *The Slave Trade, Domestic and Foreign* (1853), a long treatise by the prominent Philadelphia economist Henry Carey. Carey analyzes the conditions and causes of what he calls "slavery"—helpless, impoverished labor—around the globe, from country to country and colony to colony. His conclusion is that most of it has been brought about, and is being extended, because of British policies and activities. And such was the thesis of *English Serfdom and American Slavery* (1854), a declamatory, semi-Dickensian novel by Lucius B. Chase of Tennessee, whose villains range from the "Duchess of Sunderland" (an obvious allusion to the wealthy, philanthropic Duchess of Sutherland) to a pharisaical manufacturer-cum-abolitionist named "Solomon Greasebeans."[23]

To recapitulate, and to focus more directly upon our main theme of chattel slavery in relation to wage slavery:

American jeremiads on Britain were by no means merely a defensive *Southern* reaction to criticisms from outside of the South's "peculiar institution." They were made by Americans of all sections, and apparently of all classes. To some extent they were provoked by, and a response to, British criticisms of the United States. Among these British strictures chattel slavery was a prime target, yet was commonly linked with other "democratic" or "republican" aspects of the American polity. Americans, North as well as South, resented and attempted to rebut British charges. We thus find Americans defending chattel slavery in reaction to British criticism, who might otherwise have expressed hostility to the institution.

In addition to the tit-for-tat, retaliatory element in the Anglo-American exchanges, Britain performed the role for the United States of a negative reference group. Whatever might be said against the United States by outsiders, whatever misgivings Americans might have as to the strength and wholesomeness of their society, they could reassure themselves by referring to their stereotypes of the mother country: Britain the monarchy, controlled by the old "feudal" aristocracy and the nouveau-riche potentates of factory and counting-house. In heartening contrast, America was "republican." The term *republican* was assumed to be the complete opposite of *monarchy*. If *monarchy* symbolized privilege, hauteur, and inequality, *republic* in the American usage stood for popular sovereignty in every walk of life. This preemption of all the virtues, this consigning of the Old World to the dustbins of history, struck many British observers as an extraordinary piece of effrontery. How could Americans be so complacent? How could they possibly reject the abolitionist assertion that a nation sanctioning chattel slavery had no right to boast of American "freedom"?

One partial explanation is that in seeking to draw a boldly simple contrast between *republic* and *monarchy*, Americans interpreted both terms to suit themselves. *Monarchy* covered feudalism and industrialism, perceived as locked in an unholy alliance. *Republicanism* was on the other hand not regarded as incompatible with industrial growth, or with the accumulation of quite considerable personal wealth. Here the American escape clause was the emphasis upon the absence of the hereditary principle. According to the folklore of American republicanism, wealth was won by individual merit, not acquired through inheritance; and, having been won, by an automatic law of democratic society would be dispersed again. The process—"shirtsleeves to shirtsleeves in three generations"—was believed to be perpetual and health-giving.[24] It applied to Southerners no less than Northerners. The supposed fortune of George Washington had evaporated with his death; yet an ambitious planter such as Jefferson Davis could make a fortune in a decade or two of concentrated effort.

Moreover, since *republic* was an even more elastic term than *democracy*, most Americans experienced little difficulty in applying it to all parts of the United States. The nation, they remarked, was a confederation, and not wedded to any requirement that every state should be identical with every other. In the words of the *Southern Quarterly Review* (approvingly repeated by a Northern author), "this vast republic is made up of a number of separate, and, in many respects, independent republics, differing essentially in numbers, wealth, size and policy," though "all constituted by the solemnest compact, equals, and integral fractions of the great whole." The American republic was thus protean, capable of displaying various shapes, each, however transcendentally, "republican." Its parts could therefore include both chattel slavery and free labor.[25]

In the Anglo-American context, we can now see the manifold expedience of the controversy over chattel slavery as against wage slavery. From the American point of view it helped to cancel out and refute paternalistic British disparagements. By drawing attention to British forms of "slavery," Americans could satisfy themselves that, comparatively, chattel slavery was preferable or at least no worse. In juxtaposing "republicanism" with "monarchy," they could heighten their pride in the United States. They could also give free rein to a revolutionary rhetoric that they rarely applied to their own country. As if psychologically reenacting the emotions of the Revolutionary generation, they called out for liberty, equality, and fraternity like so many leveling radicals. The American blood boiled vicariously. American writers of quite conservative temperament seemed to be stirred into a locofoco vehemence by the spectacle of British class barriers. Indeed, a congressman in Lucius Chase's novel *English Serfdom and American Slavery* is reproached by another character, Lord Melville, for being "altogether too great a leveller." The American has been passionately holding forth on the sins of the aristocracy, and urging people like his companion: "Atone for your sins, before you lecture us! . . . Diminish your taxes. Reduce the salaries of your officers. Do not be guilty of bestowing millions upon military chieftains. Curtail the benefices of your clergy. Cut up your parks into farms. Feed your people instead of staghounds. Reduce your rents, and consider a pompous exhibition of splendor of less importance than the lives of your lower classes."[26]

How exhilarating to shout the old battle cries of revolutionary democracy, to thrust high the liberty poles, instead of having to wrangle and equivocate over painful issues of American authority, the rights of property or the sanctity of contracts! In 1842, for example, Alexander Slidell Mackenzie, the same man who had defended Jacksonian Democracy in England, was in command of a United States naval vessel, the *Somers*. Informed of an intended mutiny, Mackenzie held a court martial. Three of the supposed mutineers, a midshipman, a boatswain, and an ordinary seaman, were found guilty and immediately hanged, though the ship could have returned to port in a couple of days. The midshipman was the son of John C. Spencer, the secretary of war in President Tyler's cabinet. Mackenzie's action led to his own court martial, and to a controversy that occupied Americans for months. One of those who hotly condemned Mackenzie was the former midshipman James Fenimore Cooper. During the same period a struggle in New York State came to a head between the old patroon landlords of the Hudson valley and their tenants, the latter demanding freehold titles to their farms. In this "anti-rent war" Cooper and his fellow Democrats sided with the landlords. Both disputes were intricate. In the *Somers* affair, discipline was discipline, yet there was a suspicion that young Spencer had been victimized in part because he mingled too readily with the crew, instead of holding aloof as befitted an officer-cadet. In the anti-rent war, the landlords were not strictly aristocrats on the British model, nor were the farmers a starving peasantry. Where did right lie for a good republican?[27] It was a relief to turn from such ambiguous decisions to the clear-cut, far-off offenses said to have been committed by the mother country.

There is no reason to think that the indignation of a Cobden or a Chase was spurious. But if abolitionists perhaps made chattel slavery a surrogate for suppressed uneasiness about impoverished whites and free blacks in their own neighborhoods, it is conceivable that in assailing Britain, other Americans derived other psychological benefits. They could ease their consciences over chattel slavery, or about such disturbing features of American life as the spread of the spoils system in partisan politics, or, say, nativist riots in the cities. It is likely that Southern critiques of Northern "free society" ac-

corded with the inner sentiments of many people above
the Mason and Dixon line. Northerners too had misgivings about city violence, demagoguery, commercialism,
and the outcrop of wild reform theories or "isms." If so,
how comforting to transfer one's irritated anxiety to the
British scene. In fact, the British could be held directly
responsible for the sights that confronted Americans on
their own city streets. The Yankee who nourished a
hearty prejudice against Irish Catholic immigrants
could tell himself it was the British who, through centuries of mistreatment, had produced such an illiterate,
alcoholic, and contentious breed. Was there acute poverty in Boston or New York? It was easy to believe that
the fault lay with Britain for deliberately dumping its
paupers across the Atlantic.

At any rate, the apparent evidence convinced a remarkable number of sober citizens of the United States,
first, that wage slavery was an inherent element in the
British economy at home and throughout the British
empire; second, that the antislavery propaganda of the
aristocracy, the church, and the manufacturing or mer-
cantile interest was a calculated device to divert attention from British forms of slavery; and third, that this
propaganda concealed a diabolic plot to undermine and
even destroy the American Union.[28]

The first of these convictions we have already discussed. The second, that British antislavery sought a
diversionary scapegoat in the shape of American chattel
slavery, seemed to be corroborated by the skepticism of
British workers. They had seen through the abolitionist

scheme and could not be persuaded to swallow it; they knew that *they* were wage or white slaves, and were not to be fobbed off with sermons and handbills on the alleged sufferings of their black brothers. The theory helped, too, to explain why the great Daniel O'Connell, staunch defender of the rights of the oppressed Irish people in Parliament, also supported abolitionism. By anglophobic logic, the reason was that O'Connell had allowed his generous, libertarian instincts to be exploited; it was a further proof of the insidiousness of the British antislavery maneuvers that they should have succeeded in duping so fine a man.[29] Americans, already hostile to their native abolitionists, were additionally annoyed at the synchronizing of transatlantic antislavery activity. An American abolitionist speaker was bad enough: a British one was an intolerable affront to the national dignity. Such was the reaction to the arrival in 1834 of the voluble young English abolitionist George Thompson. He and William Lloyd Garrison had become warm friends the previous year in England. Garrison had procured for Thompson (and for Charles Stuart, another visiting British abolitionist) official invitations from the New England and American Anti-Slavery Societies, and had heralded their arrival in *The Liberator*. Garrison was particularly lyrical about Thompson. "He is coming among us," said Garrison, "as an angel of mercy. . . . The spectacle of the chivalrous Lafayette's embarkation for this country, to assist in redeeming it from a foreign yoke, has far less of sublimity in it than the high moral heroism and noble benevolence" of George Thompson.

And, said Garrison, Thompson was the finest orator he
had ever heard, surpassing even Daniel O'Connell. "His
appeals are absolutely electrifying."[30]

Garrison could not have made a more tactless introduction. He had implied that the United States stood in
need of an angelic visitation; and that the heroic Lafayette, who on his triumphal tour of 1824 had traveled
into the deep South, was morally inferior to the English
humanitarian. Another imagined slight, for antiaboli-
tionists, was the newly inaugurated Garrisonian habit of
celebrating August 1, in preference to July 4—August 1
being the anniversary of emancipation in the British
West Indies. Any abolitionist speaker would have been
risking his neck during the turbulent scenes of 1834–35.
But Thompson was especially objectionable as a British
import. A newspaper of Salem, Massachusetts, claimed
that the offense lay in exerting "improper and unconstitutional influence." A professor from Wesleyan University compared Thompson to the Roman Catholic
emissaries who were thought to be seeking to subvert
Protestant America. He added: "England is mighty only
from the retinue of slaughtered and enslaved nations in
her train; she has been for ages, and still is, a GIGANTIC
SLAVER." A Boston mob, in search of "that infamous
foreign scoundrel," seized Garrison instead, who was
probably saved from severe injury only by somebody's
shout of "He is an American!" Thompson, jailed overnight in Boston for his own safety, slipped away soon
after in a ship bound for Canada.[31]

Thompson's first sojourn in the United States, which

closed ignominiously in November 1835, was condemned by almost every section of the American public,
including the colonizationists who were still engaged in
conflict with the out-and-out abolitionists. He was alluded to in President Jackson's message to Congress in
December 1835, though not by name. Foreign interference was the nub of the complaint—as voiced, for instance, by Catharine Beecher (daughter of the Reverend
Lyman Beecher) in her *Essay on Slavery and Abolitionism*
(1837). She and others reiterated that the British had
no right to criticize an institution they had originally
brought to America. This riposte is interesting in the
familial context. Why should the sins of the parent be
visited upon the children? And if the children, accept-
ing the inevitable, have done their best to live with
it, why should the mother country persist in unjust
accusation?[32]

When Thompson came back again in 1850 he met
with a somewhat less stormy reception. Yet the same re-
sentments, the same retaliatory responses were stirred
up. A New England cartoon of the time addressed to
George Thompson, who has boasted that slavery does
not exist in his country, presents two contrasting scenes.
One is of a cheerful scene of recreation among slaves
on a Southern plantation. The other is a grim encounter
in England between a pair of artisans, a prospective
coal-miner and a factory hand. The factory worker,
hearing that his friend would have to work only four-
teen hours a day in the mines, begs for help so that he
too can "improve" his lot. And Thompson's presence in

A contrasting cartoon of chattel and wage slavery, published by J. Haven, Boston, 1850. In the upper panel, which represents in part a response to the crisis of 1850, two Southern planters comment on the cheerfully relaxed scene in front of them, while two astonished and contrite Northern visitors recognize that "we of the North have been . . . deceived by false Reports." One of the planters says: "I think our Visitors will tell a different Story when they return to the North." It would be dreadful if the Union were to be dissolved, "but we must stand up for our rights." In the lower panel the theme is "Factory Slavery." In the center, a haggard woman and her forlorn children provide the antithesis to the plump, healthy women and children of the plantation. Behind them, a military encampment is intended to suggest that the British army is a form of slavery. To the right, a corpulent pair ("Tythes" and "Taxes") symbolize the oppressive effect of clergy and landlord. At the bottom of the cartoon is a portrait of George Thompson, "The English Anti-Slavery Agitator," who was in the United States at the time. *Courtesy of the Library of Congress*

SLAVERY AS IT EXISTS IN AMERICA.

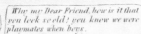

CLOTH FACTORY

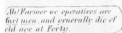

SLAVERY AS IT EXISTS IN ENGLAND.

THOMPSON
THE ENGLISH ANTI-SLAVERY AGITATOR.

various places did not go unnoticed. A mob in Springfield, Massachusetts, hung two effigies on trees at the
village green: they represented George Thompson and
John Bull.[33] In *Negro-Mania*, John Campbell described
his own and his friends' reaction to a proposed lecture
by Thompson in Philadelphia. Campbell's group ex-
plained at length to Thompson's supporters "that the
emissary of Great Britain had no right here. . . . The re-
sults were that public opinion would not sustain this man
in his attack upon our institutions and constitutions, and
he had to clear himself from our midst. I have been
highly censured by the abolitionists and their press for
preventing this man sowing the seeds of disunion in our
country and saving Philadelphia the disgrace of being
polluted by his . . . filthy language. I am satisfied . . .
that the course I pursued was both wise and just—be-
lieving as I do, in the idea, that the American people
best understand their own affairs." Thompson had recently been elected to Parliament. Campbell asserted
that "the officious interference of an English M.P. is a
piece of arrogance and impertinence" to which Americans would not submit.[34]

On the third American conviction, that there was a
deliberate British plot against the United States, the a
priori assumption was that the British had always hat-
ed the United States. The ancient monarchy could not
afford to see republicanism triumph. The Tory aristocracy and the Whig manufacturers, otherwise an improb-
able alliance, might fight one another over the repeal of
the Corn Laws; but they could combine in detestation of

America; and they could best combine, in unison with British abolitionists of less affluent stripe, by exploiting America's internal disagreements over chattel slavery. The first step, also on the face of it a little puzzling, had been the outlay of a hundred million dollars to end slavery in the British West Indies. Current and future steps might aim at provoking serious divisions within the United States, even to the extent of civil war. Alternatively, they would weaken America by encouraging miscegenation on a wide scale.

Such conspiracy theories are sometimes dismissed as paranoid. Yet in this case the argument not only ministered to hidden fears, it had a certain plausibility. The British did tend to concern themselves more closely, and in a more proprietary way, with the United States than with other nations—say, France, or Russia—who were also open to criticism on various grounds. There were evidences of British disapproval and jealousy of the United States. It was true, as Andrew Jackson contended in his 1832 veto of the bill to recharter the Bank of the United States, that a proportion of the Bank's funds were in foreign (i.e., mainly British) hands, and that British commercial policies had a considerable effect upon the American economy. In support of Jackson's veto, the *Washington Globe* (23 July 1832) listed such foreign stockholders as Viscount Gage, Sir William Keppel, and Baring Brothers, and asked: "*Is it right for Congress to legislate money . . . into the coffers of the enemies of Liberty in Great Britain?*" There were real disputes over the Canadian border in Maine and Oregon. There were reasons for suspecting that in the early 1840s the British hoped to prevent the annexation of Texas. American annexationists exploited the fact that a British abolitionist committee, accompanied by the American abolitionist Lewis Tappan, had managed to meet the British foreign secretary, Lord Aberdeen. They had proposed to him a British loan to the Republic of Texas, which was at that point bankrupt. The British government would exert pressure on Mexico to recognize Texan independence. In return, Texas would abolish slavery. The proposal got nowhere. But rumors of it, and of other kinds of British machinations, including control over a projected isthmian canal, heightened American mistrust.[35] Even the American abolitionists began to be disillusioned by the behavior of British colleagues—though of course they did not subscribe to the theory of a British anti-slavery conspiracy.[36]

Once the idea took root, it appealed to a number of different sorts of Americans, sometimes for different sorts of reasons. Nativists such as the painter, writer, and inventor Samuel F. B. Morse linked Britain with Catholic and continental European conspirators, all supposedly eager to bring about the collapse of republicanism in the United States. The writer James Kirke Paulding, in his book *Slavery in the United States* (1836), argued along the same lines as Morse. He detected a "new and more mischievous" development in the old hostility to his country. "It came masked under the semblance of humanity toward the slave."[37] Though conspiracy mania was intense in the mid-1830s, and though there was some improvement in Anglo-American diplomatic relations after the late 1840s, belief in the British plot seems to have persisted. George Thompson, whose visit in 1834/35 had been interpreted as an incident in the British plan, was still a bogey in 1851. His antagonist, John Campbell, accusing American abolitionists of "deliberate treason against our Republic," said that Thompson "also spoke in the most bitter and treasonable manner during his recent visit to our country; and there are persons born on the soil of America not ashamed to associate with such men. Cannot their machinations be seen through—is not the severance of these States the very thing aimed at . . . by the despots of Europe, so that the Kossuths, Mazzinis and McManuses shall have no spot under the canopy of Heaven to flee to?" Campbell is here hardly fair to the British, who had in fact provided asylum for numerous European liberals and radicals. But it was the abolitionist aspect that led him to lump the British with European reactionaries. "Americans," he continued, "will do well to observe how the abolitionists sympathise with each other. The tyrants of the old world are ever vigilant to destroy our form of government; and they will leave no stone unturned to accomplish their wicked . . . designs."[38]

Lucius Chase, in *English Serfdom and American Slavery*, puts the same notions in the mouths of his characters, who seem unblushingly ready to confess their evil secrets. Chase's "Duchess of Sunderland" is asked by the heroine: "What is the cause of the intense interest which you take in the affairs of the great republic?" "To wit-

ness its overthrow," is the Duchess's crisp reply, "and
thus destroy the fruitful cause of rebellion and anarchy
in Europe." In another conversation, Chase's abolitionist manufacturer "Solomon Greasebeans" explains his
position. "Why do we desert our own continent to med-
dle with the affairs of another? Why are not our sympa-
thies aroused for Russian serfs as well as for African
slaves? Why do we pass by a greater, in order to lament
a lesser evil? . . . If I was an American I should pro-
pound these questions to her grace the Duchess of Sunderland, and to every abolition society in England." The
answer, he says, would be: "Why, that we have every
thing to hope, and nothing to fear, from the example of
Russia, while we have everything to fear, and nothing to
hope, from the example of the great western Republic!"
If American abolitionists were sensible they would ponder such problems. But, Greasebeans says, "they are as
blind as bats, . . . and as full of malignant hatred towards their glorious constitution as the most inveterate
monarchists could wish." His companion queries whether Greasebeans has hopes of dissolving the American
Union. The abolitionist is utterly confident: "Why it is as
good as dissolved already, and only requires a few more
years of silent assault by British philanthropists to be
utterly and irremediably overthrown."[39]

In his book *The Slave Trade, Domestic and Foreign*
(which incidentally seems to have been an important influence upon George Fitzhugh), the economist Henry
Carey elevates the argument above the level of mere
namecalling. Yet not very far above. As Karl Marx

noted to his friend Engels, Carey's analysis was completely at odds with his previous writing in favor of free trade. Carey was now a convert to protectionism. "Now," in Marx's words, "he is singing another tune. The root of all evil is the centralising effect of big industry. But this centralising effect is England's fault again, because she turns herself into the workshop of the world, and forces all other countries back to the rudest agriculture, divorced from manufacture." Carey's ideas did not impress Marx. But as Marx recognized, Carey was a major figure in the United States; and what he was doing was to blame Britain in the name of "philanthropic socialistic anti-industrialism," though actually with the intention of promoting American industry by means of higher tariffs.[40]

We have roamed widely, and perhaps loosely, between Britain and the United States. This seemingly miscellaneous testimony, however, begins to arrange itself into patterns. None of these is of staggering novelty. The endeavor has been to show how the old Anglo-American relationship continued to be framed somewhat dramatically, indeed melodramatically, above all as a contest of rival principles, republican and monarchical. We have seen that one outcome was a tendency for Americans, in the North as much as in the South, to resent British criticisms; to retaliate by identifying wage slavery as the central institution of the parent country; to react by feeling impelled to offer at least a qualified and comparative defense of American chattel slavery; and, finally, to be willing to believe that the real threat to the United States was not slavery but dissension over slavery—this materially affected by British attitudes.

We shall look next at the career and opinions of a single American who never hesitated to present his views on all these matters, even at the risk of flagrant contradiction, yet invariably was guided by what he thought would please Uncle Sam.

THREE

Charles Edwards Lester: A Case in Point

THE PREVIOUS ARGUMENT HAS SUGGESTED THAT WAGE slavery was a prominent theme in the antebellum decades; that it was not adequately confronted on either side of the Atlantic by opponents of chattel slavery; and that the debate was further complicated by Anglo-American recrimination. We have been obliged to generalize about different regions and groups of people—"North," "South," "manufacturers," "workers," and so on—and sometimes to qualify these with "many," "some," or "most." Categorizations of this kind are often imprecise. What is more, they distort, if one's hope is to show that the distinctions between North and South, antislavery and proslavery, were in fact not always firmly established.

It is therefore useful to consider the evolution of a single person: the "Mr. Lester" identified by George Fitzhugh as a "New York abolitionist," who according to Fitzhugh "after a long and careful . . . study of the present condition of the English laboring class," admitted "he would sooner subject his child to Southern slavery, than have him to be a free laborer of England." Lester was no figment of Fitzhugh's imagination. He existed. He was, or had been, an abolitionist. Though his investigation of England was less thorough than Fitzhugh presumed, he did write copiously about the subject. He did make the avowal Fitzhugh mentioned: "I would sooner see the children of my love born to the heritage of Southern slavery, than to see them subjected to the blighting bondage of the poor English operative's life."[1] He achieved enough recognition as an author to warrant an entry in the *Dictionary of American Biography*.

At first sight his case is baffling. Charles Edwards Lester was actually a New Englander. Born in Connecticut in 1815, he was the great-grandson on his mother's side of the renowned Calvinist minister Jonathan Edwards. He himself, having been trained at a theological seminary in Auburn, New York, emerged as a Presbyterian minister in 1836. According to the *DAB* he served the church here and there in northern New York, latterly in Utica.

By 1839 Lester appears to have become an ardent abolitionist. One piece of evidence of that year is a letter by him to a fellow abolitionist, printed in Garrison's *Liberator*. It is signed "Yours in bondage, till all oppression ceases under the sun."[2] Another exhibit, also of 1839, is a small book entitled *Chains and Freedom: or, The Life and Adventures of Peter Wheeler, A Colored Man Yet Living*. This narrative, couched mainly in Wheeler's own words (or Lester's rendering of them), is a swift-paced, vivid vernacular reminiscence, though with perhaps a few "stretchers" (as Huckleberry Finn would have called them) on matters of fact. Peter Wheeler claimed to have been born into slavery in New Jersey in 1789, raised as one of the family by a kind white lady, and emancipated at his master's death, but then cheated and sold into slavery. His new master took the boy to New York State. He ran away, eluding recapture, became a seaman, and after many voyages and perils settled in New England and found religion. The tale is interspersed with pious authorial sentiments and with vehement denunciations of slaveholding. Thus, with a gloomy relish Lester pictures the dreadful fate that awaits everyone implicated in American chattel slavery on God's judgment day. "I tremble," says Lester,

to think I shall be one of its spectators. . . . And I should feel a desire to withdraw behind the throne, till the sentence has been passed upon all buyers, and sellers, and owners, of the image of the Omnipotent Judge, and executed; did I not wish to behold *all the scenes* of that great day. . . . For, as I expect to stand among that mighty company, who shall cluster around the Judgment Seat, *I do believe that God's Book will contain no page so dark . . . as that which records the story of American Slavery!* And yet I believe that that Book will embrace the history of the whole creation.[3]

Slaveholding sinners in the hands of an angry God. Is there an echo here of Lester's formidable ancestor Jonathan Edwards?

The Reverend Lester seems to have left the ministry in 1840, on the plea of ill health. He sailed for England in May 1840, arriving shortly before his twenty-fifth

birthday. Young Lester was still ostensibly an abolitionist, bent on attending the World's Anti-Slavery Convention in London. Yet his next publication, the one from
which Fitzhugh quoted, showed that Mr. Lester had
abandoned the rhetoric of his *Chains and Freedom* phase.
More precisely, he had retained the rhetoric but found
another target. Lester's new book, two volumes published at the end of 1841, bore the title *The Glory and the
Shame of England*. In the preface he explains that "the
pleasure of visiting our Father-Land; of wandering
among its venerable monuments; of conversing with its
illustrious men, was all sadly marred by the sight of the
misery, ignorance, oppression, and want I met on every
side." Then follow the words picked up by Fitzhugh,
and these: "England is a proud and wicked nation. In
her insatiate love of gain and boundless ambition for
conquest; in her unjust treatment of her dependent
colonies and foreign nations; and, above all, in her oppression of her own poor . . . people, she is without a
parallel in ancient or modern times. England has laid up
for herself a sure store of vengeance; and God will yet
visit her for her pride and wrongdoing."[4] In 1839
Southern slavery was to him the worst crime in all history. By 1841 Lester awards the palm to England, with
a corresponding shift in the Edwardsean prophecy as to
whom God will punish, come the judgment day.

Glory and Shame is not entirely a diatribe against British wage slavery. It contains some conventional tourist's
observations, for instance on the emotions aroused by
Westminster Abbey, and a hero-worshiper's account of

an interview with Charles Dickens. It extols Shakespeare, though laying claim to him as an ancestor for
Americans. It describes the opening and closing sessions
of the Anti-Slavery Convention, and praises famous antislavery spokesmen: Thomas Clarkson, Daniel O'Connell, and Lord Brougham. Lester is listed in the official
record of the Convention as "the Rev. C. E. Lester of
Bleeker Street Church, Utica," and he seems to have
made a few brief contributions to the ten full days of
discussion.[5]

Yet if *Glory and Shame* accurately reveals Lester's feelings, his chief response to England was not that of a
sightseer. His tone is far less detachedly amiable than,
say, that of Mackenzie's *American in England*, written a
few years earlier. Nor, certainly, did Lester speak as a
member of the Anglo-American abolitionist fraternity.
He reacts, rather, with righteous indignation at the contrast between Disraeli's "two nations," the rich and poor.
His outrage is conveyed in part through quotations
from British writings, including Frances Trollope's *Michael Armstrong*. Lester cites her passage on the two hundred thousand factory children "snatched away . . .
from the pure air of heaven; . . . taken and lodged amid
stench, and stunning, terrifying tumult; driven to and
fro until their little limbs bend under them; . . . the repose of a moment to be purchased only by yielding their
tender bodies to the fist, the heel, or the strap of the
overlooker!" On which Lester ironically comments:
"This is almost as shocking as anything Mrs. Trollope
found in the Domestic Manners of the Americans."[6] His

indictment embraces the woes of Ireland; the harsh effects of the Corn Laws in raising the price of bread, a staple food of the poor; the avarice of the Church of England; and British cruelty in India.

Lester's other method is to describe his encounters with casualties of the class system—ragged children, victimized women and the like—and with various people who instruct him on other evils such as the greed and immorality of the upper classes. He presents himself as a vigorous American patriot, shocked and saddened by the injustices that confront him, and convinced that unless wholesale reforms are speedily introduced, England will be plunged into revolution. "Some men," he says, "think England now more powerful than ever; but such persons forget the *wild boiling sea of smothered discontent, which is heaving under the throne and the aristocracy.*" After some months of exposure to "the oppressions and sufferings of the English people," Lester declares, "I longed to step once more upon the free soil of my childhood, and thank the God of my fathers with heartfelt gratitude that I had a free home to go to."[7] Lester thus exemplifies the good republican who has seen a contrasting society and discovered the superiority—indeed the near-perfection—of his native land. His chapters are in the form of open letters, some of them addressed to a slightly surprising miscellany of prominent Americans such as Washington Irving, John Quincy Adams, William Ellery Channing, and John C. Spencer.

More surprisingly for a supposed abolitionist, one of the letters is inscribed to John C. Calhoun. Its avowed aim is to warn Senator Calhoun, as the South's most distinguished advocate, of a British plot to raise cotton on a large scale in India. The scheme, Lester asserts, is a "bold and grand design." It appeals to the abolitionists' idea of boycotting American slave-grown cotton, the philanthropists' dream of raising the level of subsistence for India's teeming millions, the East India Company's lust for profit, the textile manufacturers' appetite for raw cotton and for world markets, and the upper class's aspirations for imperial grandeur. It is, says Lester, a union of "levellers with monopolists, and Chartists with the throne of England and her aristocracy." He takes the plan seriously, assuring Calhoun that the British have the will and the ability to accomplish whatever they set out to do.

Lester's recommendation is that the Southern planters agree upon compensated emancipation—though the idea that evil should be recompensed was of course anathema to Garrisonian abolitionists. But even with compensation, will this step not ruin plantation agriculture? Not at all, says the sanguine Mr. Lester: "the moment you perform so wise, humane, and generous an act, you will find, by experience, the superior economy of free over slave labour." Here we encounter a standard tenet of antislavery and of *laissez-faire* thought: nonslave labor is inherently more productive and more profitable than chattel labor. Hence, according to antislavery writers, the relative backwardness of the Southern economy, where the black worker has no incentive to labor effectively.[8] Lester's reasoning does not however continue in these orthodoxly inspirational terms. What is this "superior economy"? Lester explains to his imaginary planter audience that "when your labourer is free, he is on expense to you only twelve hours a day; and he will do the same work as a freeman for less money than he costs you now. And nights, rainy days, Sundays, holidays, sick-days, childhood days, and worn-out and dying days he is at his own expense, and not yours."

But this is just the objection Lester has been making to wage slavery in England—the callous disregard of what happens to the worker "nights, rainy days, Sundays, holidays, sick-days, childhood days, and worn-out and dying days." No abolitionist such as Garrison or Wendell Phillips, and few if any Northern or British exponents of the capitalist system, would refer so uncompromisingly to the circumstances of "free" labor. Is Lester then exercising his irony? Perhaps, in some peculiar, jocular, unwitting way. But there is no sign that he realizes how completely he has subverted his own logic. He continues his advice to the Southern planter: "I say farther, as long as you are a high-minded and enterprising American, who has no *cannots* or *impossibilities* in his vocabulary, you can compete with an Englishman or any other man who works for a quarter of the money that you will pay your affectionate *freeman*, attached as he would be to your person." So the free black, being in the United States, will receive the supposedly higher wages that lift the American worker above the subsistence level of the

British wage slaves. In addition, the freeman will be grateful for his emancipation, and so will faithfully serve the former master who will now be—more beneficently—his employer. The salvation lies in American enterprise and knowhow; for the American South can proceed to manufacture cotton goods out of its own raw cotton—"or bring it to the North, and we will engage to assist you. Or the wide world is open for you. Go with the fruit of your honest enterprise to any home of the great brotherhood of man, and God go with you. You are his *freemen*."[9]

Clearly, if Lester had ever been a committed abolitionist, he had ceased to be so by the end of 1841. Perhaps this almost bizarre scheme for compensated emancipation, coupled possibly with rapid industrialization for the South, was his attempt to formulate a middle position between abolitionism and something else. At any rate he never again advanced the proposal, though he was fond of incorporating previous material in his successive publications.

Whatever his intentions, Lester quickly achieved a measure of notoriety. *Glory and Shame* was published in London by the reputable firm of Bentley, and in New York under the well-established imprint of Harper and Brothers. It was quite widely reviewed in both countries. The *Southern Literary Messenger* called his book "*spiteful but interesting. . . . Mr. Lester would pick the mote out of Englishmen's eyes, whose charity begins not at home. With a pauper list which includes *one-sixth of the whole* *population* of Great Britain, she is moving heaven and earth at negro emancipation." Her *"white* negroes at home" are taxed to support West Indian emancipation.

This book . . . will be extensively read, though there is an occasional fling at the church of England that smacks of religious fanaticism. Among much wise legislation, England has been guilty . . . of much also that has proven worse than foolish. She taxed us into independence, fought us into a maritime power, and is now legislating us into a manufacturing people. Unless she changes . . . her . . . high tariff and monopolies, the day is not far distant when her Parliament will make rebels all, of her own subjects.[10]

Lester thus in the main pleased the *Southern Literary Messenger*. The London *Times*, on the other hand, was provoked into a two-part critique, stretching to some twelve thousand words. "This," said the *Times*, "is a sad, washy, trashy, snivelling and drivelling publication, a monstrous compound of vanity and weakness, of pertness and dullness, of braggardism and blackguardism, of impudence and ignorance. . . . It is a series of the most false and outrageous libels on our laws, our constitution, our morals and our religion; too pointless however," the *Times* unconvincingly professed, "to sting our pride, and too somniferous to awaken our passion."[11]

Under the pseudonym of "Libertas," Peter Brown, a middle-aged Scotsman who had recently emigrated to New York City, paid Lester an even higher backhanded compliment by immediately producing a counterblast in the shape of a whole book, *The Fame and Glory of England*

Vindicated (1842). Brown accuses Lester of plagiarism and fabrication. He ridicules Lester's assertions that prosperity and virtue reign in the United States. He blames the American speculative boom for the crash of 1837, and maintains that it has brought ruin to British bankers and manufacturers, as well as to British investors. Brown draws a picture of a British widow who has just been informed that "the interest on her Illinois state stock . . . has not been paid. . . . To enable her to send her children to a boarding-school, where they might receive a suitable education, she risked her all on the credit of the state of Illinois, as she expected to receive higher interest than in the British funds. Fatal mistake!" The British have never repudiated their debts. The American nation, however, is without honor.

Brown saves his most caustic comments for Lester's emphasis on American freedom. Praising John Quincy Adams for his fight in the House of Representatives on behalf of antislavery petitions, Brown declares:

Your republic is not yet sixty years old, and already two of the wheels are off your chariot of liberty, and your chariot lies in the dust. Freedom of speech is gone in that place [Congress], where it should ever be most sacred. Right of petition has been trampled under foot. Mr. Lester may trace the track of the car of freedom where he pleases, but he will find no trace of it in the United States. If he will search well, he will find its remains at Washington, crushed under a pile of resolutions, and held down by the force of an extra guard belonging to the Juggernaut car of slavery, which now rides triumphantly through the land.

And, as we might expect, Brown pounces upon the odd-
ity of a work by an antislavery delegate who nevertheless
"in addressing Mr. Calhoun, suddenly drops his tone of
indignation, and assumes the most humble and deferen-
tial manner. . . . He can abuse enough, when attacking
the people of other lands, but he is nearly dumb when
in the presence of the champion of slavery." [12]

Keeping up the momentum, Lester rushed into print
with another book, *The Condition and Fate of England*
(1842), dedicated to John C. Spencer, the New York
lawyer-politician whom he had also singled out in *Glory
and Shame*. His new book spared a section for a somewhat flimsy reply to Brown's attack, but otherwise reiterated and extended the charges of the previous work.
It went into a second edition in New York in 1843,
and received a certain amount of attention. It was, for
example, approvingly cited in the *Southern Literary Messenger*.[13] In general, Lester continued to press the comparison between wage and chattel slavery. His insistence
that wage slavery is far worse has, he says, not proved
palatable. The abolitionists, those "one-sided dema-
gogues," have been "greatly enraged" that he should
admit he would rather have his children brought up
under chattel slavery. He claims that he was the first
American "who had spoken so freely of the wrongs of
England." Being then an unknown author, and not
wishing "to lay too heavy a tax upon the credulity of my
readers," he had disclosed only part of the truth—an
omission he is now remedying. Even so, he was "grossly
abused" from the "editorial chair of a vile print," pre-

sumably the London *Times*. Also, in the United States he was assailed by "female editors and contributors of namby pamby magazines," who complained he had exaggerated. "Noble critics these," says Lester, getting into full stride. "Some of these persons . . . were in England, the same summer with myself. And while their pretty feet were pressing the winter carpets of the halls of the aristocracy, . . . I happened to be exploring the coal mines of Lancashire, and the factories and lanes of Preston, Manchester and Leeds. Some of these travellers have . . . described *soirées*, *balls*, and all kinds of fashionable dissipation, enough of which I witnessed to be disgusted, . . . and with descriptions of which I might have filled two volumes and peddled out the leavings to fashionable magazines, had I cared more for the esteem of the *beau monde*, than of the humane and the philanthropic."[14]

Lester had made his mark, in some sense, as we can see from Fitzhugh's awareness of him. *Glory and Shame* was reprinted in America in 1845 and again in 1850, and it was a source for John C. Cobden's *The White Slaves of England* (1853).[15] By then, however, Lester's career had moved into a new phase. In 1842 he was installed in Genoa as American consul, remaining at his post until 1847. He became engrossed in Italian history and literature, turning out a quantity of translations of Italian authors, and a substantial collaborative biography of Amerigo Vespucci (1846), the navigator after whom the American continent was named.

Lester continued to be a prolific writer. When he died in 1890 he had twenty-seven books to his credit (or, as critics like Peter Brown might have said, to his discredit). They included *My Consulship* (1853), a rambling account of his years in Italy; several biographical sketches of American artists and statesmen; a coauthored work on *The Napoleonic Dynasty* (1852); and tributes to the nation's 1876 centennial. He lived in Washington during the Civil War, commenting on events both large and small in *The Light and Dark of the Rebellion* (1863). At the close of the war he issued a considerably revised version of *The Glory and the Shame of England* (1866), which brought the tally of England's sins up to date.[16]

What is Lester's significance for us? We gather that he was a big man of extroverted personality, proud of his range of knowledge and extremely talkative. Is he simply a case of the compulsive wordsmith, "writative" as well as talkative? Did he ever have thought-out, fixed opinions, or did he merely apply his pen to whatever subject lay at hand? Is his inconstancy the reason why the youthful minister modulated so swiftly from abolitionism to the more popular pastime of twisting the English lion's tail?

We may agree that his writing never matched the eloquence of a Dickens or a Carlyle, or the profundity of an Emerson. He had no gift for sustained analysis. Much of his output is superficial, glib, and patched together with little concern for organization. His books usually seem to have been scribbled in haste and miscellaneously assembled. His notions alter in context. Thus in *Glory and Shame* he asserts that there is no sexual vice in America. In *My Consulship*, however, he contrasts the

immorality of both Britain and the United States with
the propriety of the Italians.[17] The 1866 version of *Glory
and Shame* incorporates the text of a lavishly complimen-
tary speech he gave at a literary dinner in London in
1848, the year of revolutions: "In the midst of the convulsions that are shaking other thrones to dust, England
is safe! The world can never dispense with her agency
in civilizing mankind; her commerce and her literature
are instruments God himself has appointed for eman-
cipating the world." The effect is almost laughably in-
congruous, since most of the rest of the book is an
indictment of British corruption, selfishness, and cruelty. "Until our history begins in America, it belongs to
England," says Lester with postprandial affability, "and
England's to us, as well as you. (*Cheers*). And no man
worthy of being born in either country will ever clap the
torch to that beautiful temple of harmony between the
two countries that God intended to raise, and that man
ought never to defile. (*Cheers*)."[18] Yet the very next
chapter, taken bodily from his 1841 edition, deals with
the sins of the British nobility and the distress of the
London poor. It ends: "Such is London—the West End
and Spitalfields [an East End slum]—a nobleman and a
beggar—revelry, mirth, beauty and fashion—a maniac
victim of seduction, with her dying child."

What then makes Lester tick?

One intriguing though unprovable possibility is that
in 1840, the year of his first visit to Europe, ostensibly
for reasons of health, Lester was passing through some
sort of crisis. He became married when he was only

eighteen. Not yet twenty-five when he reached England, he was already the father of two children. He could probably not have afforded to bring his family with him. Perhaps, though, he sought a relief from domesticity. The London *Times* and Peter Brown both hinted that the Reverend Lester appeared to be fascinated beyond the call of duty by unfortunate young women whom he met on the streets.[19] Such suggestions could be merely malicious. It is reasonable, however, to assume that he may have been psychosomatically rather than physically unwell. He never speaks of symptoms of illness once he is in England; indeed he keeps himself hectically busy, rushing about London, traveling north to Lancashire, Yorkshire, and Scotland. Yet he was soon to quit the ministry, perhaps with some of the self-doubts that led Ralph Waldo Emerson to take the same step.

There are curiously emotional passages in Lester's *My Consulship*, apparently jottings from a diary. "I am writing a strange kind of book," he notes at one point, "which perhaps I might just as well call my Confessions, as my Consulship." Reviewing his life in Genoa on July 15, 1844, his twenty-ninth birthday, he says: "I have fallen into a philosophical quietude, and a species of moral—I don't know what it is, but it is something worse than repose, and not so bad as stupidity—but it gives too much ease to my conscience; while I know that I have lost that *kind* of moral sensitiveness which every true and good man feels, who is living just as he ought to live." He adds wistfully, and obscurely, that while his horror of vice and his love of virtue are as powerful as

ever, "I have lost a species of . . . apprehension of the
risk of danger that I once felt." Yet "my health is perfectly
restored, and my family are well. We all love each other.
Every luxury we can think of, is in our house, and loads
our table. Our friends in America seem to love us a
great deal better than when we were with them. Nothing
looks dark, every thing seems light"—so pleasant, in
fact, that he fears their happiness cannot last: "a confes-
sion" that "discretion would never have sent . . . to the
printer."

Lester also accuses himself of having tried to do too
much. Would he, he wonders, have accomplished more
if he had sought to do less? Later in the book he puts
into direct speech the "confessions" of a person "who
passed some time under my roof." This young man
(Lester himself?) in common with other Americans had
begun life "like a candle in the nightwind, which does
not burn brightly and steadily, . . . but consumes itself
in its own wild flames." He comes to Italy "to find repose." In the young man's suppositious words: "When I
entered the ship to sail to Europe, . . . I had no disease
the physicians could name, and yet I was broken-down,
worn out. I felt as though I had lived a century. I could
hardly walk up the ship's ladder, and my friends said I
was going to Europe to die, and every one I passed
seemed sad when they looked at me; and yet I was born
with an iron constitution, and I had never been ill
enough a single day to keep to my room. I was not five-
and-twenty" (so he was exactly the same age as Lester)
"and yet I was worn out, and supposed I must die."

In these purported confessions the American finds
peace in Italy, and an escape from "the life that wears
us out at home," which

drives the young man through college and into a profession
at the age of twenty-one; and five years at the bar, in the pul-
pit, or in the counting-house, and he is broken down. This is
the life that fades out our wives, and gives them at thirty a
languid, pallid, careworn look a European woman seldom
gets: . . . this is the life that makes millions rich and poor
again in the same year; that brings on commercial panics and
convulsions: this is the life that makes our soirées boisterous
and noisy as our political meetings; that exiles quiet from our
social and domestic life, and infects every scene of home, and
family, and friends, and society, with the *business, the dollar
spirit*. How few of our countrymen know how much they lose
—how few know how much life might be made worth?

In Europe, on the other hand, the tempo is slower
and more agreeable—except for the "slave classes" of
England.[20]

If Lester had gone through a bad patch in 1840, such
subsequent comments suggest that his existence as consul and man of letters brought him plenty of gratifica-
tion. Again, they suggest that in the right circumstances
he was prepared to criticize the materialistic hurly-burly
of Yankee America in terms not very different from
those employed by Southerners like Fitzhugh and Grayson. Italy of course was not in rivalry with the United
States, unlike Britain; so Lester could afford to draw the
comparison in favor of the *dolce far niente* of pre-indus-
trial Mediterranean Europe.

The exception he explicitly makes of Britain indicates that on this subject he did maintain a consistent and persistent intensity. The English reviews of *Glory and Shame* were themselves choleric. The London *Times* said that he was no gentleman, described him as belonging "to that inferior and mongrel CASTE out of which the Lynchers . . . spring," and called his politics "ridiculous, rampant, and republican." The *Morning Post* found his book pervaded with "rabid, ranting Republicanism, and hatred of England and her institutions." The *Spectator*, though less scornful, said that *Glory and Shame* "looks more like the pious fraud of a well-intentioned zealot than the truthful exposition of a rational man looking to practical purposes and capable of forwarding them."[21] Yet the reviewers did have grounds for accusing Lester of animus.

And the tone was sustained in *The Condition and Fate of England*. Only one chapter was devoted to Peter Brown's *Fame and Glory*. The rest, running to several hundred pages, represented a piling-up of supplementary charges, almost as if he were obsessed with the theme. For the next twenty years Lester was pouring out books on other subjects. But the old anger surfaces again in his *Light and Dark of the Rebellion* (1863). In a chapter on foreign relations, Lester pays handsome tribute to Russia, "the natural ally of the United States." True, Russia's government was "a despotism in form," but it was "manifestly the only machinery strong enough to govern, protect and bless all her people." Britain, by contrast, had proved her essential falsity by declining to aid the Union in the war against the slaveholding South. "Poor fools we!" he exclaims. "Just as though the *British aristocracy* (the true name for the *British Government*) meant any thing but interference and trouble for us when her Grace the Duchess of Sutherland chaperoned the gifted Harriet Beecher Stowe through the court of her Majesty, simply because Mrs. Stowe, by writing a great dramatic novel against slavery, could be made a cat's-paw to pull the chestnuts of the British aristocracy out of the fire! Yes, abolitionism suited the purposes of the British aristocracy just *then*; and lords and ladies swarmed at negro-emancipation gatherings at Exeter Hall." These occasions were merely for show, however, so far as the aristocracy were concerned. "It did not mean any thing for human freedom. It meant hostility to the United States. *It was got up by British politicians.*" Despite the excitement over abolition in Britain in 1840, the real stimulus among the upper classes was hatred of "our *system of government*, . . . because it was a standing, growing, and luminous reproof of the blighting and degrading system of England."

Nothing has fundamentally changed in Britain, Lester asserts, from 1840 to 1863; there are still two nations, the rich and the poor. What has changed is that "British sympathy is now shifted from the slave and lavished on his master." In allowing the Confederacy to purchase war supplies in Britain, the aristocracy have stabbed the Union in the back.[22]

In the revised 1866 edition of *Glory and Shame* Lester

amplifies the accusation, embodying much of the old material from the 1841 version and lifting some paragraphs from his chapter on the subject in *The Light and Dark of the Rebellion*. The 1840 World's Anti-Slavery Convention, he reiterates, masked a "deep and well-laid scheme on the part of the politicians, to create trouble for the United States." Lester claims that he saw through the deception: "to my unpractised eye it looked at the time very much as later events have shown it,—a thorough hatred of America by the ruling classes of England."[23]

Lester changed his mind about other matters. In 1840 he was to all appearances an abolitionist. For the next two decades, the slavery that angered him was British wage slavery. He was silent during the 1850s, so far as we know, on the merits of Harriet Beecher Stowe's "great dramatic novel." With the outbreak of the American Civil War in 1861 he became convinced that the rebellion was a conspiracy fomented by the Southern planter class, first to secede from the Union and then to establish "*a colossal meridional empire*, stretching from the free States of this union towards the south, absorbing Mexico and Central America, Cuba, and all the islands of the surrounding archipelago, and appropriating all the South American states east of the Andes." Yet he spends only a few pages on this theme in *The Light and Dark of the Rebellion*. In his preface he seems to argue that the real source of America's calamity was "the merciless greed for gain." America "ran riot into every form of luxury and licentiousness which could tempt

the appetite, exalt the pride, or inflame the ambition of
our people"—phrases culled, if remotely, from the lexi-
con of great-grandfather Jonathan Edwards. In the
process, secondarily and almost incidentally, given the
decline of genuine religious sentiment in the United
States, the "subtle and deadly poison" of slavery had
flowed through the nation's arteries. "We had attempted
an impossibility. *We had tried to make Liberty and Slavery
live together in the same soil.*"[24] So liberty and slavery are
incompatible. But Lester believes that God intends the
Republic to survive and flourish. The Southern slave-
ocracy will meet with divine retribution; and so will the
even more insidious British aristocrats. Their conspiracy, in fact, seems to be more villainous. The Southern
plan, apparently, rested upon a dream of independence
without war: the British aimed at the destruction of the
whole fabric of America.

Certain other aspects of Lester's career take us further toward an understanding of him. The first is that at
the age of nineteen, in 1834, he had made a trip down
the Mississippi. Intending to spend only a few days in
what he later called "the delightful city of Natchez," he
stayed on for several months. In Natchez he met and
was fascinated by a Pennsylvania lawyer-politician, Robert J. Walker, who had arrived there a few years earlier
to join his brother in their lucrative law office. Walker
had become known as Mississippi's most effective supporter of Andrew Jackson, and in 1835 he was to conduct a successful campaign for election to the United
States Senate as a Jackson Democrat. Lester, dazzled by

this tiny, frail, energetic man, stayed on through the winter of 1834/35 to study law with him. "For what little I may have written or done . . . of any service to my fellow-men," Lester subsequently claimed, "I shall always be grateful to him as my wisest and best master."[25]

Walker could have been important to the youth in several ways. During those formative months Lester may have regarded him as a sort of ideal elder brother; Walker himself was only thirty-nine years of age. He had graduated head of his class at the University of Pennsylvania, just short of his eighteenth birthday. Lester had not attended college, and was to pass straight into a theological seminary on his return north. Conceivably, Walker suggested the step to him, as a desirable and convenient short cut to a profession. As an undergraduate Walker had boarded with a clergyman, who had loaned him money to pay the tuition.

Again, Lester may have been enthralled by Walker's capacity to adapt himself rapidly to new circumstances, including residence in the South, and to frame his justification for each move in attractive arguments. It has been said that Walker's development "abounded in contradictions." At different times, and sometimes simultaneously, he was the friend and the enemy of banks, a champion of the poor farmer and an ambitious land speculator, an expansionist pressing for the annexation of Texas and (eventually) a Free-Soiler anxious not to extend the frontiers of chattel slavery, a sharp critic of abolitionism and (it seems) a man who by 1838 had ceased to own slaves.[26] In a panegyric on Walker written in 1863 Lester said: "It is his habit to empty his fertile brain of its thoughts, . . . and then to choose the one which seems most suitable to the end required." Is that how Lester wanted to perceive himself? The eulogy of Walker continues: "Like some great magician, he pours out a multitude of gems, . . . and calls on you to select the one which most pleases your fancy, or he exercises the same choice for himself; and, . . . his store seems inexhaustible. . . . Either through the fact, by some intense activity of generalization, or by an intuitive faculty apparently independent of facts, he seems to see at a glance the great general truths which rule the economical and political world." In writing on Britain, Lester too sought to speak with the lofty assurance of one who perceives great general propositions at a glance. In retrospect, if not in 1841, Lester was clearly pleased to think that his own passionate opposition to England's Corn Laws paralleled Walker's evolution toward a modified policy of free trade. Lester believed that the repeal of the Corn Laws in 1846 had been influenced by Walker's views, and that the tariff legislation pushed through in the same year by Walker as President Polk's secretary of the treasury was part of a great evolution in the economical and political world. Walker's Unionism during the Civil War was likewise thoroughly congenial to Lester. The Northern man had come to terms with the South through long residence in Mississippi, yet in the face of secession had remained loyal to the Stars and Stripes.

From the aspiring Natchez Jacksonian of the 1830s, Lester must also have learned something about the value of political connections. We note that Lester addressed one of the open letters in the 1841 edition of *Glory and Shame* to John C. Spencer, and dedicated the next book to Spencer, "From His Humble Friend, The Author."[27] Spencer was a leading Whig politician, associated with the region of New York where Lester was involved in Presbyterianism. In 1841 Spencer became secretary of war in President Tyler's nominally Whig cabinet. The following year Lester secured the appointment as American consul in Genoa. Though he was to complain in later years of the maladministration and unrewarding conditions of the consular service,[28] he was remarkably fortunate to win the position at the age of twenty-seven. He found himself transported from a tiny house in Utica to a large house in Italy, with servants, leisure for writing, opportunities for travel, and the status of official representative of the republic of the United States. It is highly probable that he owed the appointment to John C. Spencer. Not long afterward, Spencer's political career ran into difficulty. Having been installed as Tyler's secretary of the treasury in 1843, he resigned in 1844 in disapproval of the Tyler plan to bring Texas into the Union. However, with the inauguration of the Democratic President James K. Polk of Tennessee, in 1845, Lester's old friend Robert Walker was in turn appointed secretary of the treasury. Instead of being removed with the change of administration (and of party) Lester stayed on in his Genoa consulate. The presumption is that Walker's influence was as useful as Spencer's had been.

Lester's party affiliations may have stopped short of outright campaigning. He may have hedged his bets. Thus, after the Civil War he compiled biographies both of Governor Samuel J. Tilden, a Democrat, and Senator Charles Sumner, a Republican. Nevertheless, it seems likely that through his ties with Walker he became attached to the Democrats—a preference shared, for example, by the novelist Nathaniel Hawthorne, who also received a consular appointment as the result of an old friendship.[29] If Lester did remain a Democrat of the Walker type, this too suggests why, in sympathy with the endeavors of the party, he might have tried to accommodate "Liberty and Slavery" within his personal prescription for an imperishable republic.

Let us now see where our inquiry has led. In the individual case of Charles Edwards Lester, we can perhaps conclude that he was a slapdash author, needing to earn a livelihood and also anxious—as most authors are—to achieve a reputation. What he wrote on Britain is not carefully weighed or dispassionate. His tone, as the *Southern Literary Messenger* conceded, is tinged with spite. He appears to be something like an American pugilist, eager to score points in a contest not always conducted according to the rules of fair play devised by the Marquess of Queensberry. It seems typical that he should have picked for the epigraph of *The Condition and Fate of England* some lines from an article in *Black-*

wood's Magazine on "that long sighted benevolence which sweeps the distant horizon for objects of compassion, but is as blind as a bat to the wretchedness . . . at their own doors." In putting these lines on his title page Lester announces his intent to plunge into a to-and-fro contest begun long ago.

Yet in craving recognition he is essentially no different from other writers of his day, including his hero Dickens. The art perfected by Dickens consisted of blending humor, pathos, and grandiloquence—and of choosing themes for attack about which he could be sure that majority opinion was on his side. In the United States, such opportunism crept into even the polemics over slavery. Josiah C. Nott, for example, the Alabama doctor-ethnologist who made himself an authority on supposed racial characteristics, admitted in private correspondence that his motives were mixed: "My experience has taught me that if a man wants to get on fast, he must kick up a damned fuss generally. . . . A man must get notoriety in some way or the tide will run by him." Nott candidly conceded that he craved "popularity," "money," and "professional reputation" from his publications.[30]

Also, in faulting Lester for a certain expediency in launching his attacks on England, we can still accept that the "spiteful" tone could have had ancient antecedents. He had been reared in a Congregational and Presbyterian tradition strongly antipathetic to the established Church of England. The gleam of antagonism toward the Episcopal church, manifest in his books on Britain, may have been deeply instinctual. It is arguable too that Lester found other American commentators such as Alexander Slidell Mackenzie too much in awe of the mother country, and so inclined to ignore the bad sides of the modern nation through absorption in the England of glamorous antiquity. Commenting on this, Lester said that of those few Americans who did venture any criticism, almost none thought of "looking for distress in the English cottage," i.e., in outwardly picturesque agricultural districts. Could he have been justifiably annoyed by "Republican tourists, who struggle to gain admittance to aristocratic circles abroad, . . . and who are flattered, not only out of their republicanism but their humanity"?[31]

After all, 1840 was a bad year for Britain—and an ugly spectacle for a man who had grown up in small towns where there was still in fact no great gap between rich and poor. In Britain the extremes may well have had a near-traumatic effect upon him. Unemployment exacerbated more permanent miseries. Political, social, and economic reforms were only just beginning to make an impact. The monarchy had alienated many citizens during the last years of the Hanoverians. The young Queen Victoria, reaching the throne in 1837, was as yet somewhat on probation. As Lester noted, an attempt had been made to kill the Queen in 1840. "I was in London," he recollected, close to the incident. "In passing to my lodgings late that night, I met crowds of houseless, half starved wretches coming away from the fashionable part of the town . . . around the palace. I could not but feel that . . . there were eyes which would yet see the emaciated populace thronging around that palace with other motives than curiosity, and bearing away other trophies than their own tatters."[32] Such a passage has an authentic ring. Lester seemed to sense the potential for violence, and it made him shiver.

Lester was not indifferent to Britain, any more than were his fellow Americans. The rancor he and they sometimes reveal was in part a reaction to the rude blows dealt the United States by various British commentators. In part, too, it was an ambivalent response. Lester's fulsome speech of 1848 at the London literary dinner (ironically, held in the Freemasons' Hall, where the World's Anti-Slavery Convention had met) was no doubt sincere in its way—a tribute to the feelings aroused in him by the tombs in Westminster Abbey, and by Dickens and other writers such as the poet Thomas Campbell, whom he was overjoyed to meet in 1840. The Britain he was prepared to revere, the principle of "glory" he half-wished to extol, was symbolized by its company of creative talent and of reformers. Among the latter he was even eager, not altogether consistently, to appreciate abolitionists, provided they were as hearty and open as Daniel O'Connell. Yet he felt their sympathy for his own country was flawed by paternalism and prejudice. He was dismayed when Campbell jokingly disparaged American poets in a short informal speech at the World's Convention. He must have been equally disappointed by Dickens's *American Notes*. His only printed response was that it was a "*very* small potatoe book." Only a Dickens "could afford to write such a book about such a country." [33]

In common with other Americans, Lester was relatively indulgent to Tsarist Russia, and to a France alternating uneasily between monarchy and republicanism. Just as the British devoted an almost disproportionate amount of time and energy to dissecting the United States, so did the Americans vis-à-vis the United Kingdom. The two halves of the broken family could not in his age either subsist in amity or manage to leave each other alone.

Lester, then, was no genius. He is one of a sizeable company of American authors and publicists, such as James Kirke Paulding and Nathaniel Parker Willis, who are nowadays known mainly to scholars. But he is significant for that reason. He is a representative figure even in his idiosyncrasies, since he shared these with most of his contemporaries. Paulding and Willis, for example, had both written about England; Willis to the annoyance of the London *Times*, which lumped him with Lester as a Yankee coxcomb. Paulding was as convinced as Lester of the reality of the British plot against the American republic.[34] As we have noted, even more avowedly genteel Americans like Alexander Mackenzie tended to bridle at British arrogance. The typical experience for Lester's countrymen on going to Europe was to return with the renewed conviction that America was a better place. The American sculptor Horatio Greenough, coming home in 1851 after nine years in Italy, went to look at Washington, D.C. Walking there at night, he was moved by the sight of the Capitol, lit by moonbeams and immaculately white. It was, said Greenough, "cemented with the blood of martyrs," including lovers of freedom in Europe such as Luther and Hampden and Galileo. "No man that had cast fear behind him, and done battle for the right, but had given his grain to form that temple. It stirred me." Greenough remarked that he admired much of Italy's rich heritage. "Still, I have brought from that land a fear of their doctrine and a hatred of their politics. I fear their doctrine because it seems to lull and to benumb the general, the average mind, while it rouses and spurs the few. . . . I hate their politics because they are hostile to ours."[35]

A fortiori, Lester and his kind felt the same about Britain. They were the more touchy because they were more vulnerable to British taunts. And together with Greenough they had an almost religious commitment to the American republic. This being so, they tended to treat censure of their institutions as a species of sacrilege. British criticism was peculiarly galling. Criticism from inside, of the kind voiced by the abolitionists, appeared treasonous—and doubly obnoxious when launched in concert with the old British parent-enemy.

The Unionism of America's Lesters was passionate, and on occasion incoherent and chauvinistic. How much were they beset by doubts? There is evidence, as we have seen, that they were made uneasy by the pace of American life, and the emphasis on amassing wealth. They

were troubled by irreligion. Americans such as Horace
Greeley went further, in fearing that republicanism
might become synonymous with the very vices that were
rife in Britain. Lester himself does not seem to have
been greatly concerned about the spread of American
industrialism, or that it might produce wage slavery to
compare with that of Britain. How far were their consciences stirred by the persistence of chattel slavery in a
land so fond of proclaiming its freedom?

None of these queries can be given a decisive answer.
Yet it is fairly evident that the bulk of Americans, North
and South, were perturbed rather than persuaded by
abolitionist preachments. It seems probable that, despite
intensifying sectionalist strains, even up to the brink of
secession the average American, Northern or Southern,
was more aware of things held in common than of an
irreconcilable conflict. Yearning to believe in the sound-
ness of the American republic, they were able to unite in
formulating a set of reassurances. Among these, Britain's role as scapegoat was of enormous utility. Britain
was the stronghold of wage slavery. It followed, from
the precepts of the negative reference, first, that British
wage slavery was a much greater evil than American
chattel slavery; and second, that wage or white slavery
could not be said to exist in the United States. The theory of a British conspiracy likewise served to bind together Americans of both sections, and to provide a
dramatic explanation for all sorts of disparate phenom-
ena, including the growth of an immigrant, "pauper,"
near-proletariat in America.

Lester was a writer who told Americans what they wished to hear. If home truths were overlooked in the process, then that seemed all to the good for a people devoutly eager to believe in their own destiny. Lester, in short, is a man of the antebellum American mainstream. Indeed, the term "antebellum" is of doubtful validity if our views are correct, since it implies a mutual hostility which was bound to culminate in a civil war. In truth, though some Southerners gradually became convinced that there was a fundamental and irreconcilable division between their region and that of the North, there was also a powerful commitment to the democratic, republican principles of the American polity as a whole. If Southern democracy was in some respects that of a *Herrenvolk*[36] wedded to the idea of white supremacy, this was still a selectively racial assumption widely shared with the rest of the United States. In this respect Fitzhugh, while less original than some historians have claimed, may actually have been less representative of the Southern outlook than his "New York abolitionist" source Charles Edwards Lester.[37]

Lester was editor in the late 1850s of a monthly magazine called *The Democratic Age*. For him the age, at any rate within the United States, *was* democratic. Along with most of his countrymen he seems to have had little hesitation in supposing that the citizens of Natchez and of Utica alike were brothers under the conveniently broad banner of white republican freedom. The concerns that separated them were, until the secession crisis of 1860, of less moment than the concerns that bound them together. The more reflective among them were worried, with some cause, by the looseness and stridency of American republican society. Southern intellectuals, as Drew Gilpin Faust has recently shown, were particularly prompted to ponder this problem, but they wanted to do it somewhat along the same lines as intellectuals in the North, numbers of whom yearned for a tidy, harmonious social order based on both individual and collective codes of discipline, under the tutelage of educated gentlemen.[38]

Americans of both sections could as a rule, however, agree with Lester that their nation's defects were as nothing in comparison with those of the magnificent yet maleficent mother country. On this point Lucius Chase, the ex-Congressman from Tennessee who wrote an account of the Polk administration, was in full accord with the ex-abolitionist Charles Edwards Lester of New England and New York, who had benefited substantially from the Tyler and Polk administrations. Chase and Lester expressed a considerable identity of attitude, in turn, with such other apparently different people as the Congregationalist minister Nehemiah Adams of Massachusetts, author of the amiably conservative *South-Side View of Slavery* (1854), and with the pseudonymous Ebenezer Starnes of Georgia, whose fictional *Slaveholder Abroad* (1860) attempted to show yet again how an American slave could be as shocked as his master at the spectacle of English poverty and cruelty.[39]

Lester, to repeat, was a man of the American mainstream, writing both off the top of his head and from his subconscious—and so disclosing to us lineaments of the average white American mind of the 1840s and 1850s. Superficial though he was when set against the intellectual giants of his era, Lester serves to remind us that in any era the philosophers and journalists and ordinary folk rarely manage to grapple seriously with their fundamental problems. We look for consolations or conspiracies instead of deeper, more difficult intimations. We rationalize rather than reason.

Yet, with an irony that would probably have pleased both Fitzhugh and Lester, a portion of what they innocently or confusedly asserted seems to have been in some sense acknowledged by our generation. The separate, peculiar South of historical legend has itself re-entered the political mainstream of the United States. A president from Georgia has attained the White House with the votes of Northerners as well as Southerners, blacks as well as whites. Modern scholarship accepts that wage slavery, while still a slippery concept, has been an element of profound historical importance; that class-consciousness has influenced the behavior of countless millions, not merely in Britain but round the globe; and —perplexingly, controversially, yet persuasively if we are to credit the researches of several notably unconservative historians[40]—that the chattel slavery of the South, less benign than Fitzhugh or Grayson pretended, was nevertheless more economically viable, and more robustly absorbed by its black work force, than Lester's one-time abolitionist associates could bring themselves to comprehend.

Notes

ONE—*Slavery, "Black" and "White"*

1. Fitzhugh's words on "the White Slave Trade" appear at the beginning of the first chapter of *Cannibals All! or Slaves Without Masters*. The best edition of this, edited with an introduction by C. Vann Woodward, is in the John Harvard Library (Cambridge, Mass.: Harvard University Press, 1960). Selections from Fitzhugh, with a useful introduction, can be found in Harvey Wish, ed., *Ante-Bellum* (New York: Capricorn, 1960). Wish is also the author of *George Fitzhugh, Propagandist of the Old South* (Baton Rouge: Louisiana State University Press, 1943). There is a fascinatingly appreciative analysis of Fitzhugh in Eugene D. Genovese, *The World the Slaveholders Made* (New York: Pantheon, 1969), which takes issue with Wish and with the spiritedly dismissive interpretation of the mind of the Old South in Louis B. Hartz, *The Liberal Tradition in America* (New York: Harcourt, Brace, 1955), Part 4. See too the penetrating comments in George M. Fredrickson, *The Black Image in the White Mind: The Debate on Afro-American Character and Destiny, 1817–1914* (New York: Harper & Row, 1971), pp. 59–70.

2. Grayson's poem builds upon several previous prose essays which discuss hireling and slave labor. His poem runs to 1,576 lines, of which about a quarter are reprinted in Eric L. McKitrick, ed., *Slavery Defended: The Views of the Old South* (Englewood Cliffs, N.J.: Prentice-Hall, 1963), pp. 57–68. See Thomas D. Jarrett, "The Literary Significance of William J. Grayson's *The Hireling and the Slave*," *Georgia Review* 5 (Winter 1951): 487–94; the material on Grayson (and Fitzhugh) in Edmund Wilson, *Patriotic Gore: Studies in the Literature of the Civil War* (New York: Oxford University Press, 1962), pp. 336–64; William Sumner Jenkins, *Pro-Slavery Thought in the Old South* (Chapel Hill: University of North Carolina Press, 1935), pp. 285–308; Arthur Y. Lloyd, *The Slavery Controversy, 1831–1860* (Chapel Hill: University of North Carolina Press, 1939), pp. 139–45; and Wilfred Carsel, "The Slaveholders' Indictment of Northern Wage Slavery," *Journal of Southern History* 6 (November 1940): 504–20.

3. *Cannibals All!*, ed. C. Vann Woodward, p. 109; in H. Wish, ed., *Ante-Bellum*, p. 144.

4. Wish, *George Fitzhugh*, passim. Of his contemporaries, the Southern statistician-editor James B. De Bow qualified praise for Fitzhugh by saying

that he was "like all other philosophers, a little fond of paradoxes, a little inclined to run a theory into extremes, and a little impractical." The abolitionist William Lloyd Garrison, reviewing *Sociology for the South*, described Fitzhugh as "the Don Quixote of Slavedom—only still more demented than his illustrious predecessor." These comments are cited in the introduction to Wish, ed., *Ante-Bellum*, p. 13. Louis Hartz, while recognizing the brilliance of Fitzhugh and his partial perceptiveness, sums him up (*Liberal Tradition in America*, p. 184) as "a mad genius." C. Vann Woodward sees Fitzhugh as "an individual—*sui generis*," and asserts: "There is scarcely . . . a generalization . . . normally associated with the Old South that would fit him without qualification. Fitzhugh's dissent usually arose out of his devotion to logic rather than out of sheer love of the perverse, but evidence warrants a suspicion that he took mischievous delight in his perversity and his ability to shock. He once wrote teasingly to his friend George Frederick Holmes, referring to his *Sociology for the South*, 'It sells the better because it is odd, eccentric, extravagant, and disorderly'" (introduction to *Cannibals All!*, p. x).

5. Genovese, *The World the Slaveholders Made*, pp. 118–244. But see Drew Gilpin Faust, *A Sacred Circle: The Dilemma of the Intellectual in the Old South, 1840–1860* (Baltimore: Johns Hopkins University Press, 1977), pp. 127–31, for astringent comments on Fitzhugh's standing with his contemporaries, and on the attention lavished upon Fitzhugh by Genovese among other modern scholars.

6. See for example Thomas Clarkson, *Negro Slavery. Argument, That the Colonial Slaves are better off than the British Peasantry, Answered from the Royal Jamaica Gazette*, a pamphlet reprinted from the *Christian Observer*, August 1824. The theme is explored with great learning and subtlety in David Brion Davis, *The Problem of Slavery in the Age of Revolution, 1770–1823* (Ithaca: Cornell University Press, 1975), e.g., pp. 343–73, 453. Caroline Davidson has drawn my attention to *Travels in the Western Hebrides* (London, 1793), a strongly felt account by the Rev. John Lane Buchanan, "missionary minister to the Isles from the Church Of Scotland," which contends that the Hebridean subtenantry were far worse off than West Indian slaves.

7. John Chester Miller, *The Wolf by the Ears: Thomas Jefferson and Slavery* (New York: Free Press, 1977), p. 251; Russell Kirk, *John Randolph of Roanoke* (Chicago: Regnery, 1964), p. 130; Joseph Clarke Robert, *The Road from Monticello: A Study of the Virginia Slavery Debate of 1832* (Durham, N.C.: Duke University Press, 1941), pp. 64, 67, 74, 78, 84, 85, 90; and Carl Degler, *The Other South: Southern Dissenters in the Nineteenth Century* (New York: Harper & Row, 1974), pp. 37, 48. In a letter of March 1832, Randolph argued that there must be underlings in society. The "pedestal of slavery" or its equivalent was necessary to enable equality to prevail at the upper levels. "Take your choice of slaves or *nominal* free men" (Kirk, *John Randolph*, p. 150); *Southern Literary Messenger* 9 (December 1843): 744. An almost identical counterattack is developed in "White and Black Slavery," *Southern Literary Messenger* 6 (March 1840): 193–200, a summary of recent reports on conditions across the Atlantic: "If British testimony, in relation to their own country, can be relied upon (and why not?) then we think we shall be able to demonstrate, that the operatives in the factories of England, and the poor laborers of

Ireland, are in a condition which no slave in Virginia need envy." Similar attitudes are analyzed in Robert J. Brugger, *Beverley Tucker: Head over Heart in the Old South* (Baltimore: Johns Hopkins University Press, 1978), pp. 145–47.

8. Wish, *George Fitzhugh*, supplies examples of how Abraham Lincoln and a number of other Americans were aware of Fitzhugh's publications. His theories are discussed at some length in Charles Mackay, *Life and Liberty in America*, 2 vols. (London, 1859), 2:58–72, the work of an intelligent British observer who traveled in North America in 1857–58.

9. Cecil Driver, *Tory Radical: The Life of Richard Oastler* (New York: Oxford University Press, 1946), pp. 36–55.

10. This poem, by William Taylor, was published in Stockport, near Manchester, about 1836 (Driver, *Oastler*, p. 574). On Sadler, see [Edward Gibbon Wakefield], *England and America: A Comparison of the Social and Political State of Both Nations* (New York, 1834), pp. 40–41. The *Birmingham Journal* (14 April 1833) reprinted an anonymous poem on the death of a little "factory girl" from overwork. The last stanza reads:

> That night a chariot pass'd her,
>   While on the ground she lay;
> The daughters of her master
>   An evening visit pay—
> Their tender hearts were sighing
>   As Negro wrongs were told;
> *While the white slave was dying*
>   *Who gain'd their father's gold.*

11. G. D. H. Cole, *Socialist Thought: The Forerunners, 1789–1850* (London: Macmillan & Co.; New York: St. Martin's Press, 1953), pp. 153–54, 189–94, 284.

12. Fitzhugh constantly refers to Carlyle, and took from him the title for *Cannibals All!* Emerson visited Carlyle, helped him secure publication in the United States, and corresponded frequently with him, though they grew less and less in sympathy with one another's ideas. Southern magazines, like those in the North, analyzed Carlyle's opinions in detail. See for example *Southern Quarterly Review* 18 (November 1850): 313–56, an ambitious commentary on Carlyle's *Latter-Day Pamphlets*; and "British and American Slavery," *Southern Quarterly Review* 24 (October 1853): 369–411, which praises Carlyle as "the greatest, the wisest, and the bravest living English author." Carlyle was of course Scottish. But writers of his day, on both sides of the Atlantic, often used "England" and "English" in broad senses to include Scotland and Wales and (less commonly) Ireland. I have tended to use the word "British," though without aiming at precision.

13. A previous version was published in England (London, 1842), as *The Factory System Illustrated*, by "A Factory Cripple." The author, William Dodd, apparently emigrated to Boston, having, it seems, been befriended by a wealthy Englishman. He estimates that in 1846 there were over ten thousand workers in England disabled by factory accidents. "Petition after petition has been sent into the two houses of Parliament, to the prime minister, and to the

Queen, concerning this unfortunate class of British subjects, but without effect. Had they only been *black* instead of *white*, their case would have been taken into consideration long ago. Or if they had been inhabiting any other portion of the Globe, the far-famed English philanthropists would have found them out; but because they are in England itself, under their very eye, their case is unheeded" (Boston edition, pp. 25–26). The assumption that the factory hand is a slave forms a main theme in a poem, "A Voice from the Factories," by Caroline Norton, appended to *The Laboring Classes of England*, pp. 149–68. Dodd also devotes some chapters to the agricultural laborers of England. It is worth noting that he exempts from his strictures the woollen mill of Oastler's friend John Wood, much reformed since 1830 ("A Factory Conducted on Christian Principles," pp. 94–100).

14. In her research for this book Frances Trollope met John Wood and Richard Oastler. See W. H. Chaloner, "Mrs. Trollope and the Early Factory System," *Victorian Studies* 4 (December 1960): 159–66.

15. Woodward, ed., *Cannibals All!*, pp. 149–53. The poem describes the wretchedness of a woman forced to scrape a livelihood as a seamstress. That it first appeared in *Punch* is interesting. *Punch*, established in 1841, was to become identified with British middle-class complacency. In its early years, however, its tone was often sharply satirical, and humanitarian, as befitted the 1840s. See for example an ironical cartoon, "Capital and Labour" (*Punch* 5 [1843]: 48–49), and a rather more equivocal essay, "The Reconciliation," (*Punch* 8 [1845]: 122): "The time will come when Poverty will be relieved from its serfdom. We have emancipated the slave to the colour of his skin. We have next to emancipate the slave of Poverty: to take from him the stain and blot, the blight and the disgrace of pauperism; . . . to divest him of the collar and the chain, which human pride and prejudice have, for centuries past, beheld about the neck of the Poor." For an excellent introduction and anthology see Susan and Asa Briggs, *Cap and Bell: Punch's Chronicle of English History in the Making, 1841–1861* (London: Macdonald, 1972). The reforming spirit is also revealed in Celina Fox, "The Development of Social Reportage in English Periodical Illustration during the 1840s and Early 1850s," *Past & Present*, no. 74 (February 1977), pp. 90–111.

16. Carlyle often used "Exeter Hall" as a mocking shorthand for people he regarded as sanctimonious do-gooders. Grayson's *The Hireling and the Slave* is similarly derisive:

> When Exeter expands her portals wide,
> And England's saintly coteries decide
> The proper nostrum for each evil known
> In every land on earth, except their own,
> But never heed the sufferings, wants, or sins
> At home, where all true charity begins.

There is some heavyhanded satire on "Dexeter Hall" in *English Serfdom and American Slavery* (New York, 1854), pp. 84–87, a fanciful novel by the Tennessee author and congressman Lucien B. Chase.

17. *The Liberator*, 18 December 1840. Garrison took the opportunity to answer M'Ewan in a series of vigorous footnotes. See also Aileen S. Kraditor,

Means and Ends in American Abolitionism: Garrison and his Critics on Strategy and Tactics, 1834–1850 (New York: Pantheon, 1969), pp. 244–46. Dr. Carlos Flick of Mercer University, to whom I am indebted for other references on Birmingham, has drawn my attention to a report (*Birmingham Journal*, 20 April 1833) of a public antislavery meeting in that city, under the auspices of a group of local clergy. The aim was to press for immediate uncompensated emancipation in the West Indies. The proceedings were disrupted by a large number of workers. One of them declared that "he was himself a slave in everything except the name; they were too miserable at home to assist in getting rid of slavery abroad." The proceedings were also challenged by members of the Birmingham Political Union. There was so much uproar that the meeting had to be adjourned.

18. William Thomson, *A Tradesman's Travels* (Edinburgh, 1842). Harriet Beecher Stowe's husband Calvin Stowe, who accompanied her to Scotland in 1853, launched an attack on Thomson's book in a meeting in Glasgow. George A. Shepperson, "Harriet Beecher Stowe and Scotland, 1852–53," *Scottish Historical Review* 32 (1953): 43.

19. Shepperson, "Harriet Beecher Stowe and Scotland," pp. 40–46; Frank J. Klingberg, "Harriet Beecher Stowe and Social Reform in England," *American Historical Review* 43 (1938): 549. George Reynolds, the founder of *Reynolds's Newspaper*, was the author of various novels mingling social protest and sexual titillation. One of his titles was *The Seamstress, or the White Slave of England* (1853)—followed in 1855 by *The Loves of the Harem: A Tale of Constantinople*. There is, however, no reason to doubt the genuineness of his annoyance at Mrs. Stowe.

20. For an older view see Herman Schlüter, *Lincoln, Labor and Slavery* (New York, 1913; reprint ed., New York: Russell & Russell, 1965), pp. 143–68. Corrective interpretations are offered in Royden Harrison, *Before the Socialists: Studies in Labour and Politics, 1861–1881* (London: Routledge & Kegan Paul, 1965), pp. 40–69; D. P. Crook, *The North, the South, and the Powers, 1861–1865* (New York: John Wiley, 1974), pp. 195–97; Mary Ellison, *Support for Secession: Lancashire and the American Civil War*, with an epilogue by Peter d'A. Jones (Chicago: University of Chicago Press, 1972); and Ray Boston, *British Chartists in America, 1839–1900* (Lotowa, N.J.: Rowman & Littlefield, 1971).

21. There is some evidence that Northern workers felt their own standing was impaired by the comparison with slave labor. Other evidence, however, indicates the ambiguity inherent in these comparisons. In his *Public and Private Economy* (New York, 1836), pp. 254–55, 263), the Jacksonian Democrat Theodore Sedgwick said: "Slavery had given to the common people those names of reproach which have been attached to all who profess the common man's labours. . . . In our own country, the poorest class in the free states, have sometimes been called 'white slaves'" (cited in Bernard Mandel, *Labor: Free and Slave: Workingmen and the Anti-Slavery Movement in the United States* [New York: Associated Authors, 1955], p. 64). Sedgwick implies that such opprobrium was fastened *upon* the workers, when in fact it was they who insisted on the analogy, and the employers who denied its relevance to the "free" labor force. One gains the impression, by the same token, that it was

the employers rather than the employees who were anxious to emphasize the "dignity" of labor—this being more of a semantic than a reformist consideration.

22. Brownson's essay was first published in his own periodical, the *Boston Quarterly Review*, and then separately as a pamphlet (Boston, 1840). It is reprinted in Leon Stein and Philip Taft, eds., *Religion, Reform and Revolution* (New York: Arno, 1969). The passages quoted here are in Stein and Taft, pp. 11–12.

23. Brownson's lecture is cited in Joseph Dorfman, *The Economic Mind in American Civilization, 1606–1865*, 2 vols. (New York: Viking Press, 1946), 2 : 666–67. Brownson declared to the students that it was "our duty to accept the distinction of classes as a social fact, permanent and indestructible in civilized society." There were freemen and slaves both North and South, but Southerners "call your slaves by their proper names, and . . . relieve them from the cares and burdens of freemen." Compare Carlyle's opinion, from *Past and Present* (quoted in *Southern Quarterly Review* [October 1853]: 410–11): "That I have been called by all the newspapers a 'free man' will avail me little, if my pilgrimage have ended in death and wreck. Oh, that the newspapers had called me slave, coward, fool, or what it pleased their sweet voices to name me, an I had attained not death but life! Liberty requires new definitions. . . . Brethren, we know but imperfectly yet, after ages of constitutional development, what liberty and what slavery is."

24. The New York *Free Inquirer* (6 May 1829) reports on a Philadelphia committee chaired by Mathew Carey, on the struggle for survival of seamstresses and other women workers, who were computed to have only about $16 per annum per family for food and clothing. In 1836 the Factory Girls' Association of Lowell, Mass., a mill town with reputedly almost ideal working conditions, staged a walkout to protest increases in board charges, which amounted to a wage cut of 12.5 percent. Fifteen hundred of them marched through Lowell, singing parodies of popular songs. One, to the tune of "I Won't Be a Nun," was as follows:

> Oh! Isn't it a pity that such a pretty girl as I
> Should be sent to the factory to pine away and die?
> Oh! I cannot be a slave,
> I will not be a slave,
> For I'm so fond of liberty,
> That I cannot be a slave.

This song is found in Barbara Mayer Wertheimer, *We Were There: The Story of Working Women in America* (New York: Pantheon, 1977), pp. 70–71; I owe these references to Phyllis Palmer. Seth Luther's *Address to the Working Men of New England* (Boston, 1832) is cited in Williston H. Lofton, "Abolition and Labor," *Journal of Negro History* 33 (1948): 262–63. The Lynn protest is quoted from the shoemakers' paper, *The Awl* (24 July 1844), in Norman Ware, *The Industrial Worker, 1840–1860* (Boston: Houghton Mifflin, 1924), p. 42; and see Alan Dawley, *Class and Community: The Industrial Revolution in Lynn* (Cambridge, Mass.: Harvard University Press, 1976).

25. Schlüter, *Lincoln, Labor and Slavery*, pp. 70–84; Lorman Ratner, *Powder*

Keg: Northern Opposition to the Antislavery Movement (New York: Basic Books, 1968), p. 63; Mandel, *Labor: Free and Slave*, pp. 65–95. Mandel notes that in a few cases, most flamboyantly that of the Irish-American congressman Mike Walsh, labor representatives "came perilously close to defending slavery" (pp. 81–82).

26. Lofton, "Abolition and Labor," pp. 273–76.

27. *The Phalanx* (3 November 1843), in John R. Commons et al., eds., *A Documentary History of American Industrial Society* (Cleveland, Ohio: Arthur H. Clark), 7:208.

28. *The Harbinger* (5 June 1847), in Commons, *Documentary History*, 7:217–18. *The Harbinger* was edited at Brook Farm, the communitarian colony in Massachusetts, by George Ripley. This particular piece was reprinted in at least one Southern publication, the *Planters' Banner* of Franklin, Louisiana.

29. Letter of 3 June 1845, printed in the New York *Daily Tribune* (20 June 1845) and reprinted in Commons, *Documentary History*, 7:212–13. See also Glyndon G. Van Deusen, *Horace Greeley, Nineteenth-Century Crusader* (Philadelphia: University of Pennsylvania Press, 1953), pp. 65–70; Schlüter, *Lincoln, Labor and Slavery*, pp. 50–55. Albert Brisbane, writing in the same year as Greeley, likewise presented a multiple definition of slavery: that of race or color, the "slavery of capital," slavery of the soil, military slavery, and so on. See *The Liberator* (6 June 1845), and Schlüter, pp. 49–50.

30. Cited in Joseph G. Rayback, "The American Workingman and the Antislavery Crusade," *Journal of Economic History* 3 (November 1943): 154–55. According to Rayback, James's tract ran through at least three printings. The copy held by the Library of Congress is at the time of this writing unfortunately reported missing.

31. John Campbell, *Negro-Mania* (Philadelphia: Campbell & Power, 1851; reprint ed., Miami: Mnemosyne Publishing Co., 1969), pp. 470–71.

32. Lorman Ratner, *Powder Keg*; Leonard L. Richards, *"Gentlemen of Property and Standing": Anti-Abolition Mobs in Jacksonian America* (New York: Oxford University Press, 1970). Richards suggests (pp. 131–55) that "typical" antiabolitionist demonstrators were of relatively high social and professional status, native-born, and apt to be firmly affiliated to a major political party, whereas abolitionists tended to be of lower or less established status (not, for example, members of the Episcopal church), more often foreign-born, and less often aligned with either of the two major parties.

33. Bertram Wyatt-Brown, *Lewis Tappan and the Evangelical War Against Slavery* (Cleveland: Press of Case Western Reserve University, 1969), pp. 140–41; Aileen S. Kraditor, *Means and Ends in American Abolitionism*, p. 247.

34. See the crisp, possibly too pro-Garrisonian exposition in Kraditor, *Means and Ends in American Abolitionism*, pp. 235–55; George M. Fredrickson, *The Black Image in the White Mind*, pp. 31–42; David B. Davis, "Slavery in the American Mind," in Harry P. Owens, ed., *Perspectives and Irony in American History* (Jackson: University Press of Mississippi, 1976); Ronald G. Walters, *The Antislavery Appeal: American Abolitionism after 1830* (Baltimore: Johns Hopkins University Press, 1977), pp. 111–28; and Jonathan Glickstein's valuable article, "'Poverty Is Not Slavery': American Abolitionists and the

Competitive Labor Market," in Lewis Perry and Michael Fellman, eds., *History and the Abolitionists* (Baton Rouge: Louisiana State University Press, forthcoming).

35. Walters, *Antislavery Appeal*, pp. 114–16.

36. Nathan Appleton, "the father of Lowell," originally published his articles in *Hunt's Merchants' Magazine*, and subsequently as *Labor, Its Relations in Europe and the United States Compared* (Boston, 1844). This excerpt is reprinted in *Annals of America*, vol. 7, *1841–1849: Manifest Destiny* (Chicago: Encyclopaedia Britannica, 1968), p. 164. On Phillips see Kraditor, *Means and Ends*, p. 250. The whole theme is illuminatingly examined in Howard Temperley, "Capitalism, Slavery and Ideology," *Past & Present*, no. 75 (May 1977), pp. 94–118.

37. William S. Jenkins, *Pro-Slavery Thought in the Old South*, pp. 286–87.

38. Chapter 7, "The Paradox of Poverty," and especially pp. 157–61, in David J. Rothman, *The Discovery of the Asylum: Social Order and Disorder in the New Republic* (Boston: Little, Brown, 1971), shows how Jacksonian America tended to assume that true poverty, a European phenomenon, could not exist in the United States.

TWO—*Anglo-American Discord and the Definition of Slavery*

1. See Frank Thistlethwaite, *The Anglo-American Connection in the Early Nineteenth Century* (Philadelphia: University of Pennsylvania Press, 1959), a pioneering work that covers economic relations, political radicalism, and humanitarian and educational movements.

2. A fresh treatment of this literature for 1830–60 is needed. Two older monographs are of some use: Jane Louise Mesick, *The English Traveller in America, 1785–1835* (New York: Columbia University Press, 1922); and Max Berger, *The British Traveller in America, 1836–1860* (New York: Columbia University Press, 1943). Allan Nevins, ed., *America Through British Eyes* (New York: Oxford University Press, 1948), a revised version of *American Social History as Recorded by British Travellers* (1923), is organized into too-simple categories. Thus, writings of the period 1825–45 are grouped under "Tory Condescension," those of 1840–70 under "Unbiased Portraiture." Under the former head comes Harriet Martineau, who was never a Tory; under the latter, writers such as William ("Bull Run") Russell, who was hardly unbiased. Comments in the other direction, some familiar and some less so, are anthologized in Henry S. Commager, ed., *Britain Through American Eyes* (New York: McGraw-Hill, 1974).

3. See Henry Pelling, *America and the British Left: Bright to Bevan* (New York: New York University Press, 1957); G. D. Lillibridge, *Beacon of Freedom: The Impact of American Democracy upon Great Britain, 1830–1870* (Philadelphia: University of Pennsylvania Press, 1955); and David P. Crook, *American Democracy in English Politics, 1815–1850* (New York: Oxford University Press, 1965).

4. There are examples of visits for cultural purposes in Neil Harris, *The*

Artist in American Society (New York: Braziller, 1966). On the interest in Walter Scott, see Marcus Cunliffe, *Soldiers and Civilians: The Martial Spirit in America, 1775–1865* (New York: Free Press, 1973), p. 348.

5. Cited in William Brock, "The Image of England and American Nationalism," *Journal of American Studies* 5 (December 1971): 227. Jovial specimens of the oratory of Anglo-Saxondom (his own) are supplied in George Francis Train, *Spread-Eagleism* (New York, 1859).

6. Edwin G. Burrows and Michael Wallace, "The American Revolution: The Ideology and Psychology of National Liberation," *Perspectives in American History* 6 (1972): 167–306; Winthrop D. Jordan, "Familial Politics: Thomas Paine and the Killing of the King," *Journal of American History* 60 (1973): 294–308.

7. "The old moth-eaten systems of Europe have had their day"; "The moth-eaten and age-decayed fabric of kingly government"; Whitman editorials from Brooklyn *Daily Eagle*, 1846, in Joseph L. Blau, ed., *Social Theories of Jacksonian Democracy* (New York: Liberal Arts Press, 1947), pp. 135–36. The naval officer Captain Frederick Marryat, author of *A Diary in America* (1839), was told that "in a short time England would only be known as having been the mother of America" (Berger, *British Traveller in America*, p. 62). For a lively, broad survey see Cushing Strout, *The American Image of the Old World* (New York: Harper & Row, 1963).

8. Quoted in Robert F. Dalzell, Jr., *American Participation in the Great Exhibition of 1851* (Amherst: College Press, 1960), pp. 44–55; and see Marcus Cunliffe, "America at the Great Exhibition of 1851," *American Quarterly* 3 (Summer 1951): 115–26.

9. This point is subtly developed in William R. Taylor, *Cavalier and Yankee: The Old South and the American National Character* (New York: Braziller, 1961).

10. *Punch* 13 (1847): 215. This was typical of many criticisms of the United States that stressed the incompatibility of chattel slavery and virulent anti-abolitionism, with claims for republican "freedom." See for instance the cartoon and editorial on the disruption by a mob of an abolitionist meeting in *Punch* 13 (1848): 154, and instances from *Punch* in 1851 quoted in Cunliffe, "America at the Great Exhibition." The poet William Wordsworth and the humorous essayist Sydney Smith were among the out-of-pocket British sufferers (having put their money in Pennsylvania bonds) who accused the Americans of fraud. On Smith, see Gerald Emanuel Stearn, ed., *Broken Image: Foreign Critiques of America* (New York: Random House, 1972), pp. 20–21. The usually witty Smith was on this occasion not amused. On the 1837 panic, Marryat wrote of New York: "I was in a store when a thorough-bred democrat walked in; he talked loud, and voluntarily gave it as his opinion that all this distress was the very best thing that could have happened to the country, as America would now keep all the specie and pay her English creditors with bankruptcies." In Philadelphia, he added, "the ultra-democrats have held a large public meeting, at which one of the first resolutions brought forward and agreed to was—'That they did not owe one farthing to the English people'" (Nevins, ed., *America Through British Eyes*, p. 174).

11. Sir Charles Lyell, *Travels in North America*, 2 vols. (New York, 1845),

1 : 261. Other favorable comments are noted in Berger, *British Traveller*, ch. 5 —which incidentally is almost identical with the same author's article, "American Slavery as Seen by British Visitors, 1836–1860," *Journal of Negro History* 30 (1945): 181–202.

12. Marryat cited in Berger, *British Traveller*, p. 183. And see the essays by Marcus Cunliffe (on Frances Trollope), Marghanita Laski (on Harriet Martineau), and Philip Collins (on Dickens) in Marc Pachter, ed., *Abroad in America: Visitors to the New Nation, 1776–1914* (Reading, Mass.: Addison-Wesley, and National Portrait Gallery, Smithsonian Institution, 1976). There is an excellent annotated edition of *Domestic Manners* by Donald Smalley (New York: Knopf, 1960). Arnold Goldman and John Whitley have provided a thorough edition of Dickens's *American Notes* (Harmondsworth: Penguin, 1972). After Harriet Martineau wrote *Society in America* (1837) she produced several other books on the United States; see R. K. Webb, *Harriet Martineau: A Radical Victorian* (New York: Columbia University Press, 1960).

13. Cooper's notions are delivered in a number of his novels of the 1830s and 1840s, and in such treatises as *The American Democrat* (1838). See for example the *obiter dicta* of the demagogue Steadfast Dodge in Cooper's *Homeward Bound* (1838): "I do not know that any man has a right to be peculiar in a free country. It is aristocratic, and has an air of thinking one man is better than another.... If the people cannot control ... peculiarity, or anything they dislike, one might as well live in a despotism at once." Cooper's attitudes are well analyzed in John P. McWilliams, *Political Justice in a Republic: James Fenimore Cooper's America* (Berkeley: University of California Press, 1972). His views can be set beside those of Dickens on American public opinion, as cited in Stearn, *Broken Image*, pp. 52–54.

14. Degler, *The Other South: Southern Dissenters in the Nineteenth Century* (New York: Harper & Row, 1974), pp. 88–89. Degler quotes a dialogue from a novel, *The Kentuckian in New York* (1834), by William Alexander Caruthers of Virginia. One Southerner says to another: "You know I am no *abolitionist*; ... yet I cannot deny from you and myself, that they [slaves] are an incubus upon our prosperity. This we would broadly deny, if a Yankee uttered it in our hearing; but to ourselves, we must e'en confess it."

15. Dickens's private comment to his friend William Macready is cited in Stearn, *Broken Image*, pp. 49, 292. Dickens was one of the aggrieved British authors who were the more ready to believe in American dishonesty (on the matter of payment to creditors) because of the refusal of the United States to subscribe to an international copyright agreement. The result was that the work of popular foreign authors was published without permission and without royalties.

16. Such calculations were often made by British radicals and then cited in America: see G. D. Lillibridge, *Beacon of Freedom*, p. 13. They were still current in the late nineteenth century: see Andrew Carnegie's *Triumphant Democracy* (1886).

17. Cobden's book was first published in Andover, Mass., and then in a second edition (New York, 1860). The full title is *The White Slaves of England. Compiled from Official Documents*. It has been reprinted by the Irish University Press (Shannon, Ireland: 1971). Cobden writes as an American and presum-

ably was one, though his name suggests a possible kinship with the pro-American British M.P. Richard Cobden.

18. The point is that Americans did not always concede that the testimony they used might no longer apply, or might itself have been produced as part of a campaign for reform. See William Brock, "The Image of England and American Nationalism," pp. 244–45: "For modern historians this period of British history is recognized as opening 'the age of reform.' It began with the first Factory Act, the new Poor Law, the Municipal Reform Act, and closed with the great Public Health Act of 1848. It saw investigating commissions, the use of statistics as an aid to policy and the beginnings of public responsibility for private welfare. It was the age of philosophic radicalism. Yet all this field of constructive endeavor was hidden from Americans. No American—whether public servant or man of letters—understood the transformation which was taking place."

19. Cobden, *White Slaves*, pp. 489–90; Dickens quotation in Stearn, *Broken Image*, p. 49.

20. William G. Dix, *The Unholy Alliance: An American View of the War in the East* (New York, 1855), pp. 200–202.

21. Alexander Slidell Mackenzie, *The American in England*, 2 vols. (New York, 1835), 2 : 148–55. Mackenzie (1803–48) was the brother of John Slidell, later to be Confederate commissioner in Europe, together with James Murray Mason. Their mother, whose surname Alexander adopted, was Scottish. The two Englishmen in the coach who irked Mackenzie were a Jewish banker and a businessman who had spent some time in the United States. Both criticized American manners, and both deplored Jackson's treatment of the Bank of the United States, in which they had invested money. Mackenzie remarks (2 : 154–55): "I have neither taste nor turn for argument; but, by a strange perverseness, I have a singular facility, in listening to the arguments of others, to be convinced sometimes in the directly opposite sense from what they intended. This occurred to me now, and led me first to doubt the expediency of sustaining an institution which these men were so anxious to support. The bills of the United States Bank, in which I had long been accustomed to receive my monthly pittance, were the only rag money in America for which I had any respect. What little feeling I had on the subject, had therefore been hitherto in its favour. . . . Now, however, the tide of my opinions began to turn."

22. In his final chapter, Cobden (*White Slaves*, pp. 494–95) reviews his indictment: "The crime of England lies in maintaining the slavery of a barbarous age in the middle of the nineteenth century; in keeping her slaves in physical misery, mental darkness, moral depravity, and heathenism; in carrying fire and sword into some of the loveliest regions of the earth, in order to gratify that thirst for wealth and dominion ever characteristic of an aristocracy; in forcing her slaves in India to cultivate poison [opium], and her weak neighbours of China to buy it; in plundering and oppressing the people of all her colonies; in concentrating the wealth of the United Kingdom and the dependencies in the purses of a few persons, and thus dooming all others beneath her iron rule to constant, exhausting, and unrewarded toil! We arraign her before the tribunal of justice and humanity, as the most powerful

and destructive of tyrannies; as the author of Ireland's miseries, and a course of action toward that island compared with which the dismemberment of Poland was merciful; as the remorseless conqueror of the Hindoos; as a government so oppressive that her people are flying by thousands to the shores of America to escape its inflictions!"

23. Henry C. Carey, *The Slave Trade, Domestic and Foreign: Why It Exists, and How It May Be Extinguished* (Philadelphia, 1853). The chapter-titles include "How Slavery Grows in India," "How Slavery Grows in Ireland and Scotland," and "How Slavery Grows in England." The material on Scotland (204–9) cites British sources on the responsibility of the Sutherland family for confiscating clan property, and pauperizing and expelling the crofters. Lucius B. Chase, *English Serfdom and American Slavery: Or, Ourselves—As Others See Us* (New York, 1854; reprint ed., Miami: Mnemosyne Publishing Co., 1969). An epigraph from Shakespeare on the title page reads: "Now step I forth to whip hypocrisy."

24. For a typical example, consider the remarks of Justice Story at the Massachusetts constitutional convention of 1820: "Those who are wealthy today pass to the tomb, and their children divide their estates. . . . Property is continually changing like the waves of the sea. One wave rises, and having reached its destined limits falls gently away, and is succeeded by yet another which, in its turn, breaks and dies gently on the shore. The richest man among us may be brought down to the humblest level; and the child with scarcely clothes enough to cover his nakedness may rise to the highest office in our government." Story's language ("gently" occurs twice) dwells upon how peaceful and natural the process is.

25. *Southern Quarterly Review* (January 1851), in John Campbell, *Negro-Mania* (Philadelphia, 1851), pp. 461–62; Jenkins, *Pro-Slavery Thought in the Old South*, pp. 194–96, 290–95.

26. Chase, *English Serfdom*, p. 210. Here is Chase (p. 216) on the prospect of escape to America for an English victim of the press gang and of a flogging, after his wife and eldest child have just died of cold and starvation (a full dose of fictional misery): "Two days must elapse, and then the 'Nancy Ann' would sail for the New World—a *new world* to all who have never tasted the sweets of liberty and the blessings that flow from the principle of equality—a *new world* to the victim whose spirit has been broken, and whose body has been lacerated by the rod of tyranny—a *new world* to the humbled subjects who flee with horror and dismay from the hypocritical, festering, and savage governments of the old—the *new world* of hope, and freedom, and happiness for the millions of human beings whose hearts never before throbbed but with a consciousness of suffering wrongs; wrongs that a despotic power not only thinks itself justified in committing, but without the aid of which its infamous usurpation of inalienable prerogatives would be summarily avenged." Powerful stuff. After that, it seems fussy to note that Chase's notion of the press gang is hazy. He wrongly assumes that impressment operated in peacetime and that it conscripted men into either the navy or the army. The British army, like the American, in fact relied upon recruiting adventurers, misfits, and men out of work.

27. On the Mackenzie case, see Marcus Cunliffe, *Soldiers and Civilians* (New York: Free Press, 1973), pp. 96–97; Harrison Hayford, ed., *The Somers Mutiny Affair* (Englewood Cliffs, N.J.: Prentice-Hall, 1959); and *Proceedings of the Naval Court Martial in the Case of Alexander Slidell Mackenzie* (New York: Langley, 1844). On the anti-rent imbroglio, see Henry Christman, *Tin Horns and Calico* (New York: Holt, 1945). Cooper's feelings about unscrupulous tenants and squatters are expressed in his novel *The Redskins*.

28. Nehemiah Adams, *A South-Side View of Slavery* (Boston, 1854; reprint ed., Savannah, Georgia: Beehive Press, 1974) contains elements of all three attitudes, though it is unhysterical and well-informed. Adams, a Congregational minister from Boston, made a winter visit to Georgia for reasons of health. Though some aspects of chattel slavery worried him, in general Adams found conditions appreciably better than those he had read of in England. "Pauperism is prevented by slavery. . . . Every slave has an inalienable claim in law upon his owner for support for the whole of his life. He can not be thrust into an almshouse, he can not become a vagrant, he can not beg his living, he can not be wholly neglected when he is old and decrepit." The Northern states are being flooded with immigrant paupers. Work conditions in the North are bad for some, such as the seamstresses. Adams resorts to the family metaphor to rebuke the British: "This venerable mother England . . . has only a few years since begun to reform certain dreadful oppressions . . . among her population at home, yet has seemed unwilling to allow her daughter, just come of age, a little time to dispose of one evil imposed upon us by her own hands, and which the country, as such, has no power to remove." He cites some of the British sources—Thomas Hood's "Song of the Shirt," William Howitt's *Rural Life in England*—familiar to other American commentators. And he hints that the conduct of the "venerable mother" smacks of conspiracy.

29. Leonard L. Richards, "*Gentlemen of Property and Standing,*" pp. 67–68.

30. W. P. and F. J. Garrison, *William Lloyd Garrison, 1805–1879: The Story of His Life*, 4 vols. (New York, 1885), 1:434–35. The subsequent events of Thompson's visit can be followed on into the second volume of this well-documented biography.

31. C. Duncan Rice, "The Anti-Slavery Mission of George Thompson to the United States, 1834–1835," *Journal of American Studies* 2 (April 1968): 13–31, and especially 21–28; Frank Thistlethwaite, *Anglo-American Connection*, pp. 109–11; Lorman Ratner, *Powder Keg*, pp. 39–41; Richards, "*Gentlemen of Property and Standing,*" pp. 63–65.

32. Jackson, speaking of "unconstitutional and wicked attempts" to circulate antislavery appeals through the United States mail, seemed gratified by public demonstrations "against the emissaries from foreign parts who have dared to interfere in this matter." *Garrison: The Story of His Life*, 2:73. On complaints by Catharine Beecher and others, see Ratner, *Powder Keg*, p. 35. In a "familial" sense, it may be significant that American journalists rubbed in their discovery that Thompson had once stolen money from an employer; and more significant that they derided him for being sponsored by female antislavery groups in Scotland. Frances Trollope had been dubbed "Dame"

Trollope, and portrayed as an ugly old harridan (a caricature of Mother England?). Thompson was mocked as an immature, unreliable young man dispatched on a foolish errand by Dame Britain, or rather by "canting old women," "old pussycats," "a bevy of old maids"—*old* in each of these phrases from the *New York Courier and Inquirer* (Rice, "Anti-Slavery Mission," pp. 25–28).

33. The lithographed cartoon was published in Boston in 1850. One of its English details is a sign, "SALE: A WIFE to be sold." Wife-selling was in fact not unknown, even later in the century: see Thomas Hardy's novel *The Mayor of Casterbridge*. On the ceremony in Springfield see Rice, "Anti-Slavery Mission," p. 26.

34. Campbell, *Negro-Mania*, pp. 457–58.

35. William Brock, "The Image of England and American Nationalism," pp. 233–34.

36. On these disappointments, and on the Texas issue, see Bertram Wyatt-Brown, *Lewis Tappan and the Evangelical War Against Slavery* (Cleveland: Press of Case Western Reserve University, 1969), pp. 248–68. E.g., on Tappan in London (1843): "Tappan found it agreeable to be able to censure people outside his own land for a change. True to his republican principles, he ridiculed with obvious relish the signs of aristocracy and privilege he saw" (p. 260).

37. Lorman Ratner, *Powder Keg*, pp. 36–39; Leonard L. Richards, *"Gentlemen of Property and Standing,"* pp. 62–69, 116–18.

38. Campbell, *Negro-Mania*, pp. 487–88.

39. Chase, *English Serfdom*, pp. 173, 230–31. George Sawyer, a Louisiana lawyer, has a similarly low view of American abolitionists—"hypocrites, disunionists, and traitors, willing to be used as a cat's-paw, in the hand of England; . . . like Judas of old, to betray the pride and glory of America into the hands of its enemies" (*Southern Institutes* [Philadelphia, 1858], p. 286).

40. Marx to Engels, 14 June 1853 (London), in Karl Marx and Frederick Engels, *Selected Correspondence, 1846–1895*, trans. Dona Torr (New York: International Publishers, 1942), pp. 68–71. Carey's book was published in England as *Slavery At Home And Abroad*, a less misleading title than the American one. On Carey's route toward protectionism, see Joseph Dorfman, *The Economic Mind in American Civilization, 1606–1865*, 2 vols. (New York: Viking Press, 1946), 2:799–805. Carey was wealthy, well known, and the recipient of an honorary degree from New York University.

THREE—*Charles Edwards Lester: A Case in Point*

1. C. Edwards Lester, *The Glory and the Shame of England*, 2 vols. (New York: Harper, 1841), 1:viii.

2. *The Liberator*, 15 November 1839. The letter, from West Stockbridge, Mass., is addressed to John A. Collins. A kind of pep-talk to abolitionists at a time when they are suffering setbacks and intense disapproval, it urges them as "children of faith" to put their trust "in the power of Freedom's God."

3. *Chains and Freedom* . . ., by "the Author of the 'Mountain Wild Flower'" (New York, 1839), pp. 163–64.

4. Lester, *Glory and Shame*, 1 : viii–ix.

5. *Proceedings of the General Antislavery Convention, 12–23 June 1840* (London, 1841); *The Antislavery Reporter* (17 June 1840), pp. 124–38. These and other references, e.g., to British reviews of *Glory and Shame*, are the result of valuable research undertaken for me long ago by Peter d'A. Jones.

6. Lester, *Glory and Shame*, 1 : 167–68. Lester repeats the jibe (2 : 260) in a section on the extent of prostitution in England: "I . . . wish that Mrs. Trollope would write a book on the domestic manners of the English."

7. Lester, *Glory and Shame*, 2 : 288, 281–282.

8. Howard Temperley, "Capitalism, Slavery and Ideology," *Past & Present* no. 75 (May 1977), pp. 106–11; and see Barry W. Higman, *Slave Population and Economy in Jamaica* (Cambridge: University Press, 1977).

9. Lester, *Glory and Shame*, 2 : 50–52. These references are to the New York edition (the pagination is different in the London edition).

10. *Southern Literary Messenger* 7 (December 1841): 874–75. In the early 1840s this periodical commented angrily and at some length on British arrogance and dislike of the United States, as exhibited by the abolitionists; by Dickens in his *American Notes* and his novel *Martin Chuzzlewit*; by the insistence of British navalists on the right of search; by Lord Palmerston's contemptuous allusion to the American flag as "a piece of bunting"; and by British demands for an international copyright agreement. See for example "Our Relations with England," *SLM* 8 (June 1842): 380–96, and "Speculations upon the Consequences of a War with Great Britain," *SLM* 8 (July 1842): 444–46, this last a reply to an article in *Fraser's Magazine*, "War with America a Blessing to Mankind."

11. *Times*, 25 and 31 December 1841. Each part of the review ran to about six thousand words.

12. Libertas [pseud.], *The Fame and Glory of England Vindicated* (New York, 1842), pp. 63–66, 268–269, 199. Brown also observes (p. 10): "It is said he was one of the deputation from the United States to the World's Convention. . . . The author informs us that he was present at some of the meetings, . . . and gives some account of their proceedings, but he does not say in what capacity he attended. But . . . it is evident . . . that the object of his journey was to make out a case of gross oppression, by the British Government, and deep degradation, and misery of the people, in order to show to the gaze of an admiring world, the free institutions, and perfect happiness of the people of the United States. American Slavery is seldom introduced, and when it is, our author employs language so guarded and submissive, as might serve as a model for an experienced courtier." Peter Brown (1784?–1863), formerly a merchant in Edinburgh, came to the United States in 1838. In New York he contributed to a pro-British paper, the *Albion*, and then founded the *British Chronicle*. He moved to Toronto in 1843, and soon joined with his son George Brown in establishing the Toronto *Globe*. See the *Dictionary of Canadian Biography*, s.v. "Brown, Peter."

13. *Southern Literary Messenger* 9 (December 1843): 742–43.

14. Lester, *The Condition and Fate of England*, 2 vols. (New York, 1842), 1:254, 276–277.

15. Cobden, *White Slaves*, p. 105, cites Lester as "an author of reputation."

16. *Dictionary of American Biography*, s.v. "Lester, C. Edwards."

17. Lester, *Glory and Shame*, 2:259–60; idem, *My Consulship*, 2 vols. (New York, 1853), 1:85–86: "I have been in upwards of fifty Italian cities, and I can say of every one of them, what no Englishman, and no American can say of any one city in their countries: I never saw . . . in an Italian city, what can be seen in Regent street or Broadway every morning, and every afternoon, and every evening, and every night—painted women, walking the streets, dressed in the height of fashion, alone—brazen-faced—impudent."

18. Lester, *Glory and Shame*, (1866 edition), 1:194–200.

19. "While he was acting the part of the 'friend of humanity' in England, his virtue was four times at least in more imminent danger than his faithful Gertrude [his wife] would have approved of " (*Times*, 25 December 1841). Brown (*Fame and Glory*, pp. 11–12) describes Lester's meeting with a pretty girl in Liverpool "who offers him *a companion*. Our Rev. author . . . asks, whether it is a gentleman or a lady, when the . . . girl replies with a smile that it is a companion 'more intelligent than a gentleman, and less troublesome than a lady.' Having delivered this speech, . . . she proceeds to offer him a book, called 'The Railway Companion.'"

20. Lester, *My Consulship*, 1: 108–11, 266–69.

21. *Times*, 25 December 1841; London *Morning Post*, 14 December 1841; London *Spectator*, 11 December 1841.

22. Lester, *The Light and Dark of the Rebellion* (Philadelphia, 1863), 65–77.

23. Lester, *Glory and Shame* (1866 edition), 1:181.

24. Lester, *Light and Dark of the Rebellion*, pp. 180–82, 9–10.

25. Lester's acquaintance with Walker, and the panegyric that follows, are presented in *Light and Dark of the Rebellion*, pp. 88–93.

26. The complexities of Walker are summarized in Glyndon G. Van Deusen, *The Jacksonian Era, 1828–1848* (New York: Harper, 1959), 198–99. Other details can be found in the *Dictionary of American Biography*, s.v. "Walker, Robert J."

27. Lester, *Glory and Shame*, 2:230. Addressing Spencer, Lester says: "As a member of the Legislature and Speaker of the House of Assembly of your own state; in the National Congress; as a lawyer and jurist; and as Secretary of State for New-York, you have been alike eminent for patriotism, learning, and a deep regard for the interests of the people." This sounds like a citation for an honorary degree.

28. Lester, *My Consulship*, 2:262–312.

29. The biographies of Tilden and Sumner were published in 1876 and 1874 respectively. Lester had also published a life of Sam Houston in 1855. Hawthorne's old friend from college days at Bowdoin, was President Franklin Pierce, for whom he produced a campaign biography. On Hawthorne's political rewards, see Marcus Cunliffe, *American Presidents and the Presidency*, 2nd ed. (New York: McGraw-Hill, 1976), p. 129.

30. On Nott, see Ralph E. Morrow, "The Proslavery Argument Revisited," *Mississippi Valley Historical Review* 47 (1961): 92. Nott was the author, among other works, of *Two Lectures on the Natural History of the Caucasian and Negro Races* (Mobile, 1844).

31. Lester, *Condition and Fate of England*, 1:253. In fairness to Lester, we should stress that in the circles he mixed in the notion of a British conspiracy was in the air, though his gloss on the commercial feasibility of Southern emancipation was his own. How such theories moved to and fro across the Atlantic is illustrated by an article from the *Natchez Free Trader* (quoted in *Glory and Shame*, 1841 edition, 2:46). The article, itself a commentary on a meeting held in Manchester to discuss the cultivation of cotton in India, was then, according to Lester, read aloud at the World's Anti-Slavery Convention. The Convention spent some time in deploring the forms of slavery imposed on workers in British India. George Thompson was one of the British abolitionists who also condemned his country's policies in India. Lester may perhaps be forgiven for wondering which aim was uppermost in the minds of some of the British antislavery leaders—helping the Indian peasantry, or injuring the plantation South.

32. Lester, *Condition and Fate of England*, 2:238.

33. On Campbell (who later apologized for his joke), see Lester, *Glory and Shame*, 2:86–92. Campbell was particularly admired by Americans for his poem "Gertrude of Wyoming," on an atrocity perpetrated by Indians under British command during the War of Independence. On Dickens, see *My Consulship*, 1:33—a note from Lester's diary of 5 December 1842.

34. On Paulding, see Louis Filler, *The Crusade Against Slavery, 1830–1860* (New York: Harper & Row, 1960), pp. 89–90; Ratner, *Powder Keg*, p. 38; and Richards, "*Gentlemen of Property and Standing*," pp. 68, 71. Willis (see the *Dictionary of American Biography*, s.v. "Willis, Nathaniel Parker") was not a believer in British conspiracies, and did not hold strong opinions about politics or economics. Yale-educated, dandyish in appearance and literary style, he spent a good deal of time in London and was widely known in Europe for his travel sketches. An English lady endorsed him as "more like one of the best of our peers' sons than a rough republican." However, the articles he sent back to the *New-York Mirror* (later published as *Pencillings By the Way*) were thought indiscreet, and cost him most of his English friends.

35. Horatio Greenough, *Form and Function*, ed. Harold A. Small (Berkeley: University of California Press, 1957), pp. 36–37. This extract is from Greenough's essay "Aesthetics at Washington," first published in *The Memorial of Horatio Greenough*, ed. Henry T. Tuckerman (New York, 1853). While in Italy he had executed a large seated figure of George Washington, commissioned by Congress. Though it was for Greenough a labor of patriotic love, the sculpture (now in the Smithsonian's Museum of History and Technology) was much criticized for portraying the Father of His Country half-nude in a toga. Another reaction comparable to that of Lester can be found in William Ware, *Sketches of European Capitals* (Boston, 1851): see the excerpt in Henry S. Commager, ed., *Britain Through American Eyes* (London, The Bodley Head, 1974), 286–89. Ware, a New Englander and one-time Unitarian minister, shared the view of other Americans that commercial and manu-

facturing wealth had become "the real nobility" in England: hence the unity of attitude between the landed aristocracy and the *nouveaux riches*. The English, said Ware, were indignant at the continuance of American slavery, but complacently indifferent to worse conditions in India, or indeed at home. The privileged classes were sanctimoniously eager to offer up prayers for the poor—"yet seamstresses, the Spitalfield weavers, the weavers and spinners in Manchester and Glasgow, and especially the innumerable slaves of the slopshop [or sweatshop], live in misery and die in want."

36. "The overwhelming majority of antebellum Southerners, it should be recalled, either owned no slaves or were farmers who owned only a few." Such men were "for intraracial purposes . . . fiercely democratic in their political and social thinking, strongly opposed to any formal recognition of the principle of aristocracy among whites." Fredrickson, *The Black Image in the White Mind*, pp. 66–67. Fredrickson (p. 61) follows the sociologist Pierre L. van den Berghe in defining *Herrenvolk* democracies as regimes like the United States and South Africa, whose white democracy has rested upon a theory of subordination for other peoples.

37. See the persuasive statement in Drew Gilpin Faust, *A Sacred Circle: The Dilemma of the Intellectual in the Old South, 1840–1860* (Baltimore: Johns Hopkins University Press, 1977), 127–30. Faust, who takes issue with the analysis of Fitzhugh in Genovese, *The World the Slaveholders Made*, argues both that Fitzhugh came late to the slavery debate, using themes developed by others, and that his writings were ultimately a source of annoyance to intellectuals like George Frederick Holmes, a professor at the University of Virginia whom Fitzhugh regarded as a friend and mentor.

38. "The men of mind who constructed slavery's defense sought a plausible belief system for their society. . . . Thus they based their arguments upon moral and social values to which large numbers of Americans both North and South could assent. Stewardship, which Genovese defines as the essential principle of the master-slave relationship, was an important characteristic of the evangelicalism that pervaded all of nineteenth-century America and much of England as well. Historians have particularly emphasized its efficacy in the North, where it served as a motivating force behind the myriad of reform movements. . . . Indeed, self-conscious fears about growing materialism and declining morality were . . . national rather than peculiarly Southern." Faust, *A Sacred Circle*, p. 130. Faust's "circle" consisted of five close friends: the novelist William Gilmore Simms, the agriculturalist Edmund Ruffin, the politician James Henry Hammond, and the professors Nathaniel Beverley Tucker (also author of a pessimistic novel, *The Partisan Leader*) and George Frederick Holmes. The preachments and the occasionally querulous paternalism of the Northern clerisy are examined in Clifford S. Griffin, *Their Brothers' Keepers: Moral Stewardship in the United States, 1800–1865* (New Brunswick: Rutgers University Press, 1960) and in the first section of George M. Fredrickson, *The Inner Civil War: Northern Intellectuals and the Crisis of the Union* (New York: Harper & Row, 1965). On the political alignments that often cut across sectional considerations, see Joel H. Silbey, "The Civil War Synthesis in American Political History," *Civil War History* 10

(October 1964): 130–40. This is of course not to deny that slavery versus free soil became an intensely combative issue: see for instance the analysis in Rush Welter, *The Mind of America, 1820–1860* (New York: Columbia University Press, 1975), pp. 344–87. Without such antagonism, the breaking of the Union in 1860–61 becomes impossible to explain. The attitudes of men like Lester, however, help us to understand why that crisis took so many Americans by surprise, and why they were disposed to interpret what had happened as the outcome of British and Southern (or Black Republican) plots against the old Union.

39. The full title of this work is *The Slaveholder Abroad; or, Billy Buck's Visit, with his Master, to England. A series of letters from Dr Pleasant Jones to Major Joseph Jones of Georgia* (Philadelphia, 1860). "Ebenezer Starnes," the supposed presenter of these letters, which refer to the period 1851–53, was a pseudonym for William Tappan Thompson (1812–82), an Ohio-born Georgia journalist-editor. Thompson's career is sketched in the *Dictionary of American Biography*. See also Howard Temperley, *British Antislavery, 1833–1870* (London: Longman, 1972), p. 71, which suggests that the book might have been partly inspired by Fitzhugh's *Cannibals All!* Temperley provides much other interesting detail, for example on the visits of George Thompson to America and of Harriet Beecher Stowe to Great Britain. In *The Slaveholder Abroad*, pp. 62–70, Dr. Jones takes Billy Buck to an Exeter Hall meeting attended by Harriet Beecher Stowe and her husband. Billy, indignant at the slanders he hears on American slavery, reproaches an English lady for having stolen blacks from Africa in the first place, and then for condoning the poverty and cruelty of life in England: "How come, ef da so sorry for poor nigger, da no sorry for poor buckra [white]? . . . How come dem buckra men killee da wife, dem wife killee da husband, an dem moser killee da chile? I want know dat! Heh? How come da no gib ebely body nuff to eat? Heh? You come to Georgy, Missis; ebely body got plenty to eat da, an nobody hurt wimins an chil'n." Billy is referring to the many excerpts in the book, from English newspapers, of trials for murder and brutality. *The Slaveholder Abroad* also cites English testimony on cases of swindling, theft and political bribery. The condition of laborers in heavy industry is not directly documented. Billy Buck, however, scornfully rejects an attempt to persuade him to run away from his master and secure employment as a hodman, or brick-carrier in the building trade, and the author reproduces editorials from the London *Observer* (14 March 1853) and the *Times* (19 May 1853), entitled "The White Slave in England" (the unprotected female) and "English Seamstress Slavery" (pp. 298–99, 365–67). "Surely," says the *Times*, after describing the arduous drudgery of young milliners, "this is a terrible state of things, and one which claims the anxious consideration of the ladies of England who have pronounced themselves so loudly against the horrors of negro slavery in the United States. Had this system of oppression against persons of their own sex been really exercised in New Orleans," instead of London, they would have been swift to express their outrage.

40. See for instance Wilhelm Backhaus, *Marx, Engels und die Sklaverei* (Düsseldorf: Pädagogischer Verlag Schwann, 1974); Edward P. Thompson,

The Making of the English Working Class (New York: Pantheon, 1964); John W. Blassingame, *The Slave Community: Plantation Life in the Antebellum South* (New York: Oxford University Press, 1973); Robert W. Fogel and Stanley Engerman, *Time on the Cross*, 2 vols. (Boston: Little, Brown 1974); Leslie Howard Owens, *This Species of Property: Slave Life and Culture in the Old South* (New York: Oxford University Press, 1976); and Herbert Gutman, *The Black Family in Slavery and Freedom, 1750–1925* (New York: Pantheon, 1976).

Index